Don't Buy Software for Business Until You Read this Book.

A guide to choosing the right software for your company & achieving a rapid return on your investment.

Author

K.N. Kukoyi

Don't Buy Software for Your Small Business Until You Read this Book.

A guide to choosing the right software for your company & achieving a rapid return on your investment.

OTHER BOOKS BY K.N. KUKOYI

Develop Your Idea! Get off to a flying start with your startup. Guided exercises & resources for exploring & validating new business ventures.
Got a business idea in mind? Let's test it out! Plan for success with the Develop Your Idea! book, an Amazon 5* rated best seller purchased by entrepreneurs in 12 countries. Research your business idea using the guided exercises, templates and resources provided.

Amazon.com reviews for Develop Your Idea!
"If you're considering a startup, the author shares a common goal and is looking to encourage and help you through the pre-startup process. I have had experience starting two software as a service companies...and I found very solid and practical advice in this book regarding how to go about validating your product idea and your potential customers...it is an easy and concise read."

Available at your local Amazon store, or via this universal link for all countries: http://mybook.to/Develop-Your-Idea-exercises-validating-ebook

*   *   *

Don't Hire a Software Developer Until You Read this Book. The handbook for tech startups & entrepreneurs (from idea, to build, to product launch and everything in between)
A best-seller in multiple business categories and multiple countries including the UK, US, Canada, Brazil and Australia, this is *the* software survival guide for startups, small businesses and entrepreneurs that want to start, or grow their tech business the smart way.
Learn what you need to know and do to get your software product built and successfully delivered into the hands of your customers.

Amazon.com reviews for Don't Hire a Software Developer Until You Read this Book
"The only problem with this book is that it didn't come sooner. As an entrepreneur who went through this process blind, I can tell you that this book is a must have for any business in this day and age. This book would have

prevented me from several mistakes that cost $$$. I recommend that you read this book from cover to cover—an ounce of prevention is worth a pound of cure!"

Universal link for all countries: http://myBook.to/Dont-Hire-Software-Developer-Until-ebook

Both books are available in 13 Amazon marketplaces: the UK, US, Canada, Australia, Netherlands, Brazil, France, Germany, Spain, Italy, Japan, India and Mexico.

RESOURCES

There are a number of resources that are provided free with this book. Here's the full list, including links:

1. **Business requirements assessment**. (Chapter 2.)

   Word document version and Excel version with MoSCoW prioritisation:
   http://bit.ly/resource1-assessment.

2. **Total Cost of Ownership budget spreadsheet**. (Chapter 5):
   http://bit.ly/resource2-TCO.

3. **Parking Lot template**. (Chapter 7): http://bit.ly/resource3-parkinglot.

4. **Product comparison and shortlist spreadsheet**. (Chapters 7 & 8):
   http://bit.ly/resource4-comparison-shortlist

5. **Clarification Questions PDF**. (Chapter 8): http://bit.ly/resource5-clarification.

6. **Trello boards** that you can copy and adapt for your own use:
   www.bit.ly/manage-priorities-online
   www.bit.ly/trello-customer-service

7. **Business report:** In their Own Words: *SME Challenges & Trends Survey, 2017.*
   The first report of its kind for years, this qualitative survey engaged the directors, CEOs and managers of UK-based SMEs. Discover the frustrations, challenges and successes experienced by businesses like yours in this report about modern business life.
   www.bit.ly/report-resource7

DEDICATION

For Irene.

Thanks to all those that provided their input and feedback. It has been very much appreciated.

I would also like to thank the people that highlighted the need for this information to be shared.

Your feedback led to the creation of this book.

ACKNOWLEDGEMENTS

With thanks to Claire Walsh, who provided her expert opinion on some of the legal matters covered in this book.

Claire Walsh CIPP/E
https://www.linkedin.com/in/claire-walsh-64316a1b/?ppe=1

CONTENTS

SECTION 1

CONSIDERATION

CHAPTER 1

Origins

"It is not the strongest or the most intelligent who will survive, but those who can best manage change."

- Charles Darwin

Summer 2006

Wimbledon, London.

We had just said goodbye to the fourth software vendor that had come to present their CRM system to us.

Having shown them to the lifts, our team reconvened to exchange feedback.

What was the verdict so far?

There were the systems that we felt we would outgrow quickly, those that were too rigid and inflexible, the behemoth "oil tanker" products that we feared would drive our business, rather than our business driving them, and a whole host of other eccentricities; and that was just the software!

Then there were the consultants and software vendors.

We saw the full gamut; from the wet-behind-the ears newbies, to the archetypal slick salesmen; sharp-suited, shoes shined, giving perfectly polished answers to our questions, but whose smiles did not reach their eyes. Having delivered their pitch countless times, they were professional, but nevertheless, were going through the motions.

We were planning an ambitious multi-million pound build / buy combination, intending to integrate the software product that the Agile software delivery team I was part of had designed and built from scratch, with software able to guide us in adopting best-practice standards in customer relationship management.

Despite experiencing every stage of growth and transition you can imagine, our business, (started by two entrepreneurs in the mid '80s) had reached a stage where we had in-house technical experience to draw upon when making technical decisions, and a solid software selection process in place.

Our hybrid product was successfully rolled-out in phases to our business users based in North America, Europe, the Middle-East and Australasia and it received praise from City of London analysts.

Spring 2016

Fast forward 10 years and my company, Purposeful Products had sponsored a business research project based on trends and challenges in the SME sector.

The output was a report called *In Their Own Words,* and in a departure from the usual statistics crunched out for multiple-choice surveys, participants' opinions were captured in the form of quotes.

CEOs, managers, heads of departments and directors were interviewed; all employed by small and medium-sized enterprises with between 5 and 200 employees.

The survey highlighted the challenges faced by SMEs when trying to find suitable software and suppliers to meet their needs.

This group of businesses was a random sample, spanning 11 different industrial sectors, yet the majority had either recently bought, or were planning to buy some form of software in the coming months.

These UK based companies were in the market to buy a range of software solutions including those for email, knowledge management, finance, CRM (Customer Relationship Management), ERP (Enterprise Resource Planning), MIS (Management Information System) and BI (Business Intelligence), often without significant in-house IT expertise or guidance to support their decision making.

Whether you consider it a blessing or a curse, technological innovation is now a part of everyday life, and touches almost every business. Companies are under increasing pressure to keep pace with changes and to maximise the opportunities that it presents. To opt out is to fall behind.

These are some of the comments made by the SMEs that were interviewed:

"Eighteen months ago, we invested in a CRM that turned out to be complete rubbish." CEO, Membership Organisation

"The only thing that keeps us sane is knowing it's not just us going through these [technology related] issues." Director of Marketing, Retail Sales

"At the moment, we're overhauling all our business processes... We're investing in purchasing new systems and keeping up with technological changes." IT Manager, Recruitment Company A

In addition to the level of investment in IT evident amongst the businesses that took part in the survey, there was also frustration stemming from negative experiences with large consultancies and software vendors. Participants felt that these companies did not understand how to work effectively with them.

"Software is a continual challenge...With every project that doesn't go well, I wonder what could have been done differently. I wonder if they [the consultancies] do the same." Managing Director, Recruitment Company B

This added an extra layer of complexity to the quest to find the right software and secure a return on the investment made.

Current Trends

Were the findings from the *In Their Own Words* survey unusual?

I don't believe they were.

In fact, they mirror several global trends that have become evident in recent years:

- The *Gartner Group*, the world's leading information technology research firm, has reported that businesses without formal or mature IT departments are increasingly making software purchasing decisions without technical advice. This also applies to individual departments within businesses that have their own budgets to spend as they wish.
- Investment in cloud-based services is still increasing, representing a significant change in IT spending patterns.
- Large software companies see SMEs as the next market to tap into, with Deloitte, PwC and other professional service firms developing new products, and collaborating with software suppliers to bring new solutions to the small business software market.

To quote *Accountancy Age*, providers of business and finance news: *"With around 125 million SMEs worldwide, responsible for around 65% of business employment, it's a lucrative space."*

Finances Online, a Business to Business directory agree, stating that: *"Small and medium businesses continue to drive SaaS growth fuelled by CRM, business analytics, and storage solutions."*

Deriving value from software can be a complex process, and companies attempting to purchase business software without prior experience, or technical counsel face numerous challenges.

To get the best end result, it is important not just to "go through" the software purchasing process, but to *manage* it.

It is essential that anyone purchasing business software understands the wider implications of their decisions, beyond simply finding software that meets immediate needs and preferences.

Why read this book?

Allow me to clarify what I meant when I spoke of *managing* the process a few moments ago.

In addition to researching and identifying products based on their business requirements, purchasers of software may need to evaluate add-ons and extras, and vet (and later coordinate, and monitor) prospective vendors or 3rd party suppliers.

Then there are finance and budgetary implications, the estimating of future growth and scalability requirements, and the coordination of training and change management activities to minimise the disruption that replacing software systems can bring.

There will also be contracts to review and negotiate, industry rules and business regulations to contemplate, security, storage of data, and other matters to consider... and the responsibility for achieving a return on the investment made!

Not only is there a lot to consider, but it is a sign of the times that these decisions now need to be made more frequently.

Today, companies both large and small are playing an inescapable game of catch-up to keep pace with technological advances. Even the smallest businesses have several types of software in place, and the cycle of continually replacing and upgrading systems and acquiring increasingly more advanced tools has already begun.

Would you agree that understanding how to buy software that delivers the desired results has become an important business skill?

Ten years on from sitting on my first software selection panel, information on how to navigate the software purchasing minefield is *still* not widely available. My interviews with SMEs confirm that this remains a risky, expensive and challenging process.

Depending on the size of your business, you may not have a project management function to track, manage and hold all the parties involved accountable, an experienced IT function to guide you in IT strategy, a legal, or procurement function to manage tenders, review paperwork and negotiate terms, or business analysts to gather requirements, review and document your business processes, research the options available and present the facts to you, so you can make an informed decision!

The objective of this book is to ensure that software purchasing projects are set up for success. Making well-informed decisions will enable buyers to gain the maximum benefit from the products purchased, even if they do not have access to any of the aforementioned resources.

As someone who has been hired to work on projects after the first (or even second) attempt has gone wrong, and to work in teams formed to replace software that businesses can no longer tolerate, I have gained a lot of insight into the mistakes that businesses make and the *buyer's remorse* faced once problems start to surface!

As you read through this book, I will explain the points at which the software selection process can go wrong, and the preventative measures that you can take. We'll discuss a range of tips, techniques, and methods to avoid the pitfalls that businesses encounter, and the mistakes commonly made during the software purchasing process.

You can follow the information in each chapter step-by-step, or select from the tools and tips provided as you see fit.

Who am I?

I began my IT Career in 2004 and since then have worked on a number of multi-million pound projects to create, implement and integrate software, including websites, online software applications and mobile apps.

My experience spans across business, as well as "tech", including: software delivery, business analysis, process mapping, market research and product development.

I have researched and recommended off-the-shelf products, written business cases for the purchase of new software, and project managed the delivery of products purchased from suppliers, as well as software built from scratch whilst following *Agile* principles.

My consultancy, Purposeful Products supports small businesses in managing software and process-related challenges.

Having led and worked in teams that build software for clients, sat on committees and panels to select software products, and managed 3rd party relationships with software suppliers on behalf of clients, I appreciate the challenges that businesses face when choosing and rolling out new software systems.

This is my third book for entrepreneurs and small businesses.

In my experience, the most common issues and complaints with software are that it:

- Is found to be missing important features. Unfortunately, this means that the purchasing process will need to be repeated in the short to medium term.
- Ticks the right boxes "on paper," but in practice is difficult or time-consuming to understand and operate.
- Does not complete tasks or processes to a high enough standard, or execute them in the specific ways that the business wants.
- Does not meet essential criteria relating to security, performance, auditing, reliability or other similar requirements.
- Does not help your business to meet legal or regulatory requirements, leaving the business open to fines, sanctions or even legal action.
- Is incompatible with other software systems that are in use, and will not integrate with them.
- Cannot actually be purchased because of internal opposition, or disagreements!

I will explain the reasoning you may wish to apply as you search for software that meets your needs, and I'll give you the IT insider's view, highlighting important details that suppliers may not be eager to divulge.

What topics will be covered in this book?

Here's what will be covered and where you will be able to find the information:

In Chapter 2, you'll find a **business requirements assessment** and several tools to help you clarify what you need your software to do, and to prioritise functionality. This stage of the process is critical, and has many pitfalls - I'll point these out to you as we go along.

Is it best to **build, lease or buy software?**
Should you buy **enterprise software** or a **SaaS (Software as a Service) solution?**
When should you choose the **public cloud vs. the private cloud** and **hosted vs. self-hosted options?**
In addition to this, what kind of **software licensing options** exist?
We will review each option in turn, along with the relevant advantages and disadvantages, and key points to consider in Chapters 3 and 4.

Companies are often unaware of the **hidden costs, add-ons and extras** that can come with buying new software, so we'll talk about putting together a budget, and we'll explore the *true* cost of purchasing your software in Chapter 5.

Business legislation and regulations can affect the choice of software that you can reasonably consider. You will find information about this in Chapter 6, along with resources and guidance documents to help businesses improve their IT Security, and protect themselves and their customers against fraud.

You will also notice that additional information is provided in the **Ask the Expert** commentary boxes. This information has been provided to shed light on some of the topics we will be covering from the perspective of a legal professional - always useful when considering commercial contracts and IT law!

In Chapter 7, we'll discuss **6 steps** to consider when carrying out **product research,** and the key things to look out for when reviewing the software available on the open market.

Due diligence is important, and this should include vetting both products *and* service providers. It is important to choose a supplier whose terms do not restrict you unfairly, and can deliver a high standard of service. Asking the right questions when speaking to consultancies, 3rd party suppliers and software vendors, is crucial. The questions, tips and resources provided in Chapters 8 and 9 have been provided to assist you with these matters.

In Chapter 10, we'll discuss some simple **project management** and **risk management techniques** that will help you manage risks and prevent issues from arising, or escalating, and at the end of the book you will find a list of free and low-cost software products suitable for SMEs.

I promised to provide you with information about ways to get a **solid return on your investment, (ROI) as quickly as possible,** and I intend to deliver!

Your chances of achieving a good ROI improve or decline with every decision you make, starting with your initial research, so we'll review some important considerations that businesses tend to overlook.

Complementary spreadsheets and templates have also been provided for your convenience. You will find them in the relevant chapters, and in the Resources section at the start of this book.

You can contact me with questions and feedback at:
hello@purposefulgroup.com
http://www.purposefulgroup.com/contact-us.html.

With my best wishes,
K.N. Kukoyi

References

Gartner Says by 2020 "Cloud Shift" Will Affect More Than $1 Trillion in IT Spending. http://www.gartner.com/newsroom/id/3384720

Accountancy Age. *Deloitte Propels into the SME Market.*
https://www.accountancyage.com/2016/06/22/deloitte-propels-into-sme-market-with-2-5m-accounting-services-investment/

Accountancy Age. *PwC to target global SME market with Sage tie-up.*
https://www.accountancyage.com/aa/news/2426432/pwc-to-target-global-sme-market-with-sage-tie-up

Finances Online. *2016 SaaS Industry Market Report: Key Global Trends & Growth Forecasts.*
https://financesonline.com/2016-saas-industry-market-report-key-global-trends-growth-forecasts/

The Financial Times. *Deloitte Targets SMEs with Cloud Based Service.* https://www.ft.com/content/ac2c8ec8-36f2-11e6-9a05-82a9b15a8ee7

Purposeful Products. *In Their Own Words: SME challenges and Trends Survey, 2017.*
www.bit.ly/report-resource7

CHAPTER 2

Laying the foundations: identifying priorities and avoiding pitfalls

"Things which matter most must never be at the mercy of things which matter least."
— Johann Wolfgang von Goethe

Have you ever heard friends or colleagues complain about the terrible software they are forced to use at work?
The story is often the same: no-one understands how to use it properly, it's terribly slow, doesn't do what it should, or the steps required to complete tasks have been arranged in such an illogical manner, that the sanity of the people that built it is frequently called into question!

In many businesses, there is an active grapevine between current and former employees.
Is this something that you have experienced?

Everything is dissected, from the pros and cons of the "old" office environment vs. the "new", to the quality of the computer systems offered by employers. Staff, recognising the value of the systems in place compare notes, wary of employers known to use poor-quality software applications.

No-one sets out to choose a product that becomes a burden to the organisation or department that uses it, or has the power to scare off new recruits - so how does this happen?

We'll explore the reasons in this chapter, and if you complete the exercises provided, you will have a set of prioritised software requirements that can be used to benchmark any products that you might consider purchasing.

Get clarity on what the criteria for a pass, or fail will be, so that you are guided towards tools that will be an asset, and not a liability. Give this stage of the process the attention it deserves and you will reap the benefits.

Once you have established the features and criteria that are important to you as a business, these requirements will act as a compass of sorts to steer you in the right direction. They can also be handed off to a project manager, agency, software house or consultancy for further discussion.

Let's get back to looking at why companies end up with poor quality software.

What goes wrong during the software selection process?

Mistakes made early in the software selection process can cause plans to stall, or fail, and may damage your chances of achieving a return on your investment. Common errors include:

Failing to allocate sufficient thinking time to the process, and not asking enough of the right questions.
This applies to the questions that your business or department *asks of itself,* as well as the questions asked of the companies competing to supply your software.
When internal requirements are not reviewed in enough detail and criteria are not tight enough, software that should never have made it onto your shortlist will appear suitable.
Without a thorough review of your processes and requirements, certain products may seem appropriate when considered at face value, and it may not be obvious which ones will be best for you. This is often where problems begin.

Not having a clear plan.
Replacing or upgrading software is a project and should be treated as such.

This means preparing:

1. Written selection criteria that describe your requirements and what you want to achieve.
2. A method for benchmarking products, so you can draw comparisons between products.
3. A selection process that outlines the steps you will to take to reach your goal.
4. A system for tracking potential and actual costs and expenses relating to the software.

This doesn't have to be painful - I have provided templates that you can use throughout this book - look out for the download links.

We will address point 1 in this chapter, and you will find information to support you with points 2, 3 and 4 in Chapters 5 to 8.

Project pitfall

Don't go shopping without a "shopping list"!

Being in the market for software without quality selection criteria is much the same as shopping without a list - you risk coming away with all manner of non-essentials that seem like a good idea at the time. However, you may forget critical items that should have been a priority.

Not vetting, or considering the supplier as well as the product.

Understanding the capability of the supplier to deliver their services, the range of services offered, and the disadvantages and limitations of these services is also important before you proceed.

Avoid products or suppliers that will pull you out of alignment with your goals.

Service providers should be responsive and able to meet your needs in terms of compliance, security and management of your data, among other tasks and you may well become reliant upon 3rd parties to perform these activities for you.

If you love a product, but have concerns about the provider of the service, proceeding may be risky unless you can obtain the product from another supplier.

Allowing singular modes of thinking to drive the selection process.
Cover your bases by including people who will consider the big picture and those who will pick up on important details during the software selection process.
If you have too much emphasis on big picture thinking, the vision may be clear, but the details of how to reach it, or what is needed to reach it may be missing.
In contrast, too much focus on particular functionality, or specific details will lead to decisions being made based on these items, to the exclusion of other essential characteristics that a product or vendor should have.
The wider implications for the *entire* business with respect to matters such as security, contractual agreements and compliance must not be overlooked.
In order to make the best decisions, you will need to consider both.

Underutilising the skills and expertise of staff.
Inclusion does not mean letting others make decisions for you, but it *should* lead to the selection of a quality product.
The involvement of additional people is sometimes avoided because "decision by committee" can be challenging - but this *can* work well.
A committee, selection panel or forum that represents a range of interests and priorities also shows that efforts are being made to consult others, and will help you make well-informed decisions.
Draw on the assets you have available, because the knowledge, skills and perspectives of your staff can be excellent resources!
Involve the people who use the current software on a regular basis and understand the processes well, and allow them to help you reach the right conclusions.

Consider every team, department or person who will be buying, using, supporting, or benefitting from the software as a stakeholder, (and consult with your legal, finance, security and compliance teams if you have access to these resources.)

The importance of winning "hearts and minds" is not appreciated.
Your personal style will also have an impact on the project.
If you're a very "task oriented" person, it can be easy to overlook the fact that *people* will play a huge role in your business obtaining a good return on its investment.

If people feel excluded, do not feel heard, or fear that important items are being overlooked, you may face internal struggles and resistance to your plans.

Non-cooperation may come in many forms - objections, lacklustre performance, obstructive behaviour, refusal to contribute to the funding of the software required, or withdrawing or withholding support that would be beneficial to the project.

Even if you are in a position of authority, remember that other people can still make your goals harder to accomplish.

Additionally, people who feel that they have no stake in the process will be less enthusiastic and motivated about your proposals.

An appreciation of *why* new tools are needed, *why* this is a positive event and *how* the business, and staff at all levels of your organisation will benefit is important if you value the support, goodwill and cooperation of your colleagues.

Change can be very disorientating for some people, and you may need to handle the reactions that can arise in response to it. In particular:

- Fear of the unknown. *Why is this happening? This could be a disaster!*
- Fear of losing existing, familiar tools and processes. *This works fine, why change anything? Will the new software do X, Y and Z for us? If it doesn't, I am <u>not</u> going to support this!*
- Demoralisation / demotivation may accompany the perception that changes have been introduced without warning. *No-one asked me! All I do is work here, why would my opinion matter?!*

How damaging do you think these modes of thinking might be to your project?

Although you may disagree with these attitudes, be vigilant, consider what people within your business are saying and be prepared to address issues and deal with any concerns and negativity relating to your proposals. It is in your best interest to do so!

Not making tough calls when necessary.
On the other hand, there *will* be some hard decisions to make, and it

will be difficult to select the right product if you get bogged down in trying to please everyone!

If you have considered the different needs of your business, then you will be best placed to make a judgement call, bearing all the relevant points in mind.

Some evaluation and prioritisation techniques appear later in this chapter to assist you when making difficult choices.

Businesses also get "caught out" by *unknown unknowns*, things they aren't even *aware* are important, due to a lack of experience with purchasing software.
Therefore, in Chapter 8, we'll run through a set of questions that you can ask software vendors and service providers.

*   *   *

Gathering your written selection criteria

Begin with the end in mind!

Habit #2 in Stephen R. Covey's book, *The 7 Habits of Highly Effective People* is an excellent mantra to consider during the software selection process. A review of your business and its objectives is an important activity to undertake before going out to market to look for a new product. Consider the following questions:

- *What is driving you to consider new business tools?*

- *What are the most important problems that you wish to solve, and the benefits that are most worthy of pursuit?*

- *How will you know when you've achieved your objectives?*

Your answers will highlight what you must get back from your investment and why. They will also help you to verify that your software is producing the expected returns.

In this section, you will find an assessment that I designed for customers. It allows me to gain a deeper understanding of my clients' businesses, and an insight into what each business *really* needs its systems to do.

This assessment will be suitable whether you are buying software for a whole organisation, team, or department. To cover all the bases, it considers big picture strategy, as well as more detailed day-to-day processes. It will also help you to identify your "deal-breakers."

A key factor in achieving ROI is focusing on, and prioritising the right things.

If the product you buy doesn't support you in achieving the goals, and solving the problems that you identified as being important, then you will have bought the wrong software.

Remember that if you consider the questions carefully, and then stick by your criteria, it will become difficult to buy the *wrong* product!

The business requirements assessment covers the following topics:

1. Overview. Where are you now?
2. Tasks and processes
3. Departmental / Team requirements
4. Goals and targets
5. Your customers
6. Risk management
7. Data storage and management
8. Software integration
9. Reporting and analytics
10. Employees and expansion plans
11. Success / failure criteria
12. Identifying your top "must haves" in terms of specific benefits sought... and your deal-breakers.

Delegating tasks

You can complete the assessments and exercises in this book yourself, or hand them over to the people best placed to manage them. Be sure to ask them to really think about the questions that are being asked and to provide detailed responses.

Collecting information and feedback

This information could also be gathered via a series of group workshops or brainstorming sessions that focus on the specific needs of each group, or department and capture all their key requirements and activities.

You may also wish to request feedback using a survey. The following tools will allow you to create a survey for free, or at a very low cost:

SurveyMonkey, https://www.surveymonkey.co.uk/.

Typeform, https://www.typeform.com/pricing/.

Google Forms, https://www.google.com/forms/about/.

SurveyGizmo, https://www.surveygizmo.com/plans-pricing/.

I have gathered internal feedback in questionnaire format for clients, and this approach can yield a lot of great insights. However, you will need to nominate someone to collect, analyse and write up the findings.

Before starting, you'll need:
- A digital or paper based method for capturing your thoughts.
- To allocate some uninterrupted concentration time to complete the exercise. Split the assessment across several shorter "power sessions" if it is difficult to find a single block of time to complete it.

Instructions:
- Run through the assessment and note down your answers in the context of the software that you are considering, the challenges you face, and the benefits you are seeking.
- Highlight the questions that need further consideration or investigation, and return to them later. Some may feel more applicable to your organisation than others. In that case, please focus on those that are most relevant.

Bear in mind that the questions that are hardest to answer may be the most important!

You can download a copy of the full business requirements assessment in XLS and Word formats here: http://bit.ly/resource1-assessment.

The assessment questions

1. Overview

- What do you *do well* as a business, department or team?
- What must you continue to do well?
- What do you need to do *better*; for example, faster, more accurately, in higher volumes, or to a higher standard? [Insert other relevant areas of focus as needed.]
- Please state the *tasks or processes* that require the *most* improvement and why, and what changes, or activities would improve them.
- When considering your *internal processes* as a [business, department or team], do you need to focus more on improving *efficiency (doing things right)*, or *effectiveness (doing the right things)*? (Both are important, but which is *most* relevant to your business at this time?)
- How could software help you improve your *efficiency, or effectiveness*? (Could it support staff in performing the right activities, in the right way, or at the right time? How could it help to maximise performance in important areas?)

Fig 1 - Efficiency vs. effectiveness grid.

RIGHT THINGS, WRONG WAYS	RIGHT THINGS, RIGHT WAYS
SURVIVE	THRIVE
WRONG THINGS, WRONG WAYS	WRONG THINGS, RIGHT WAYS
DIE QUICKLY	DIE SLOWLY

- What **challenges, concerns and issues** does your business, department or team face on a regular basis?
- Which of these are **most** damaging, costly, time-consuming, or problematic?
- *New software could help us **maximise our strengths** as a [business, department or team] and amplify the effect of the things that are working well / that we do well by:*

  _____.
- *New software could help us **reduce issues, resolve problems** and **minimise our weaknesses** by: _____.*

2. Tasks and processes

It is possible to end up with "holes" in your business processes if all the duties that staff need to perform and the tasks that your new software must perform for you are not fully accounted for. List the activities performed by each department, or team and the steps involved in each process from start to finish, including the following information:

1. Identify the steps needed to complete each business process that your new software will need to support. (*Start by looking at how things work with your current system and note any process related changes or improvements you'd like to see in the new one.*)
2. Identify where data originates from and where it flows to and any output that you expect.
3. Identify which activities belong to each team, department or job role so it is clear who does what, as well as any interdependencies and any hand-offs between teams or different job functions.
4. What options should staff have when performing their activities and what decisions do they need to make?
5. Where does the process end? What happens then?
6. If the process then moves into another system, (or involves or progresses on to another team) please note this down.
7. Will these team(s) rely on systems or software to perform any other tasks? Please write these down.
8. Which laws, or regulations do staff need to follow as they complete each business process?

You may wish to capture each process in writing, using numbered lists, diagrams, or process flow charts if you are comfortable with these. Using diagrams can make it much easier to share, and accurately communicate information about your processes.

Fig 2 - This example demonstrates a more complex process improvement chart, created using LucidChart. https://www.lucidchart.com.

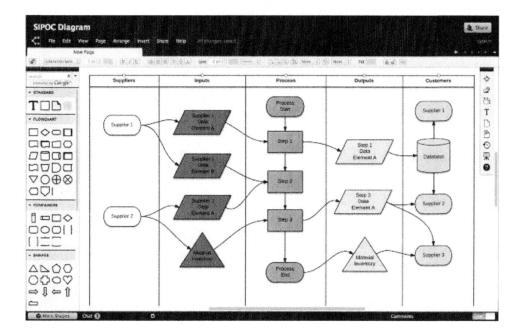

- *Name of process, or activity _____.*
- Steps involved in the process, including any important information from the 7 points above _____.
- Are there any steps in your processes, or any activities you're hoping to adjust, or eliminate with the introduction of new software? What changes would you like to see?
- Do you need the new software to help staff complete tasks in a particular order or in a specific way? If different from above, please write down your requirements.

Repeat this process for each department, or team as needed.

3. Departmental / Team requirements

Department / Team [insert name]:

- Wants software to do _____ [list your requirements], for reasons: _____.
- Wants software to do _____ [list your requirements], for reasons: _____.

Repeat this process for each department, or team as needed.

may become a priority. Software that does not work well on smartphones or tablets could create challenges for staff trying to perform their normal duties.

4. Goals and targets

- In the next 12 months, as a [business, department or team], we want to have / be / achieve _____.
- We wish to *save / reduce costs* in _____ by £/$/€ _____ per _____ by (date) _____.
- We will achieve this by _____.
- We want to *increase sales / revenue / profits / output* by £/$/€ _____ per _____ by (date) _____.
  We will achieve this by _____.
- New software will assist us in achieving these goals by _____.
- Given my comments so far, I / we see our business, department or team's performance improving through the use of software in the following areas: _____ and through these additional changes, or improvements _____.
- Based on our answers, we'd like to see a return on our investment within _____ and we expect this to come from the following source(s) / in the form of; _____.

In the downloadable template, you will have space to insert your own time line(s) and extra information as needed.

5. Customers

- Our customers have asked us to *start* doing

  _____.

- Our customers expect us to do *more*

  _____.

- Our customers want us to *stop* doing

  _____.

- We could *add more value* for our customers by

  _____.

6. Risk management

- The things that trouble me as a leader and concern us as a [business, department or team] are: _____.

- The events or activities we want to *prevent, or discourage* as a [business, department or team] are:
_____.

- The *risks, or threats* we face as a [business, department or team] are _____ and we *most strongly* wish to avoid _____. (Consider lawsuits, security issues, data loss, data theft, non-compliance with laws and regulations, fines, bad press and other risks that your business is exposed to. Consider that the technology choices you make may expose you to *all* these risks.)

- The *compliance requirements* for our business are _____, in order to comply with _____ regulations / legislation / rules.

- How should your software support or enhance compliance? (We will cover topics related to compliance in more detail in Chapter 6.)

- Other *compliance requirements* for our business are _____ in order to comply with _____ / legislation / rules.

- Security requirements to be met are:
_____.

7. Data storage and management

- What sorts of data / records / information will your software need to store? _____ , _____ , _____ .
- Where does this data come from?
_____.

8. Software integration

What other systems or software do you want your new software to communicate with (push data to, or pull data from)?

_____.

Name the types of data and the systems involved.

9. Reporting and analytics

* As a company, we would like to have more data / knowledge about _____because it would help us

  _____.

* We will need reports every _____ which contain information about _____, _____, _____ to satisfy the requirements of _____ [name the people, departments, or teams].

How important is data for tasks such as business planning, forecasting, and understanding the trends and cycles within your business, department or team?

10. Employees, and expansion plans

* As a business, department or team, we'd have happier staff if

  _____.

* We'd be able to attract more high-calibre staff as a [business, department or team] if _____.

* New software could relieve these issues by

  _____.

* As a business, department or team, we expect to grow by _____in the next 6 months.

* As a business, department or team, we expect to grow by _____in the next 12 months.

* As a business, department or team, we expect to grow by _____in the next 24 months.

Answer these questions for each department or team as needed.

11. Success / failure criteria

Make sure that your success / failure criteria are accounted for in the requirements for your new software. They provide additional (and valid) ways of expressing, and monitoring your ROI – in other words, do the problems you wanted to get rid of disappear and do you experience, or observe the positive changes you had hoped for?

As a business, department or team, after buying / building the software, I / we will be disappointed if:

- We still have to / are *still* doing / haven't been able to stop doing
  _____, _____, _____ .

- The following things: _____, _____, _____ have not improved / are *still* a problem.

- We're not doing *less* _____, _____ , _____.
- Our *competitors* are still _____ , _____,_____.

- We are unable to do *more* _____, _____ , _____.
- We haven't *succeeded* in _____, _____ , _____.

You have now gathered information across a number of important topics. Together they will help you cover your bases, so you can more easily identify and select the right software.

Is there any conflict between the answers you gave, and your *existing* business goals for the next 12 - 36 months?

If so, make any necessary amendments, so that team or departmental goals, business strategy and software requirements are all in alignment.

Your software should support your strategy!

12. Identifying your top business "must haves" and benefits… and your deal-breakers.

Considering the answers that you have provided during this assessment, what are the top 5-10 benefits your new software MUST deliver for your business, department or team?

1.

2.

3.

4.

5.

You may add more rows to the documents provided if you need to.

What about your non-negotiables, restrictions and deal-breakers?

Knowing the points which you are (and aren't) prepared to negotiate on will be very helpful when trying to identify suitable software.

We *won't* consider any software that does not do / have the following:

1.

2.

3.

4.

5.

You may add more rows/items if you wish and I would expect that your list will grow initially.

A copy of these questions is available here: http://bit.ly/resource1-assessment.

The more requirements you have, the more important it will be to organise them and set clear priorities, so we'll consider this in the next section.

Prioritising your requirements

After completing the *Business Requirements Assessment,* you may have a lot of information and requirements.

Now you'll need to decide on the most pressing needs, balancing different priorities, whilst staying true to your strategic vision. You'll also need to work within the boundaries of any legal or regulatory constraints and other business deal-breakers that have been identified.

For this reason, we will cover several techniques to help with prioritisation; The *5 Whys* and *MoSCoW.*

The 5 Whys

The *5 Whys* exercise was invented by Sakichi Toyoda, the founder of Toyota Industries, known for their *Lean* methods of production.

It is a simple, but powerful tool used by business analysts, developers and engineers for problem solving, troubleshooting and getting to the root-cause of issues. It is also used in the *Analyze phase* of *Six Sigma,* a methodology used to aid process improvement.

Use this technique if you have a large number of requirements to prioritise, or have some tough decisions to make.

It is easy to simplify requirements into sound-bites and say "we must do

this, or we must do that..."

For instance, an employee might say:

"It is critical that the system can do **X** for us." But w*hy* is this activity, or process so important?

The 5 Whys process is a simple one. Start with the initial statement:

"It is critical that the system can do **X** for us."

Then ask:

Why is that important?

Take the answer given, and ask again:

Why is that important?

Take the answer given, and ask again:

Why is that important?

Take the answer given, and ask again:

Why is that important?

Take the answer given, and ask again:

Why is that important?

The end-point is the root-cause of the problem, or "fundamental truth" about X

By the time you reach the 5th why (or sometimes earlier) you'll have reached the heart of the matter. You can then decide whether the item, X is essential, or not.

MoSCoW

MoSCoW is a great prioritisation tool.

It is used widely in Agile software development to help both the clients requesting the software and the teams delivering it to remain focused, and to manage the scope of projects.

It is a tool I use frequently when working with clients to clarify where time and effort should be allocated on projects. However, it can be used for any tasks or activities.

MoSCoW consists of four *prioritisation categories*; *Must, Should, Could* and *Won't*.

Must. This category is for core work that *must* be done.

Your "musts" should always be high-value, high-benefit items.

This list should include your essential *functional requirements*. These are core, integral pieces of functionality that a new product would be useless (or have limited value) without, and your *non-functional requirements,* which are not things that the software should *do,* but characteristics that it must have and boundaries, standards or constraints it should be bound by, such as those related to security, performance and compliance.

Should. These are your important, but non-essential requirements.

Could. You *could* benefit from these things. Some of them will be "nice to haves" or just ideas that you've come up with that may, or may not be of significant value.

Won't. There has been an agreement that your software definitely *won't* include these items, or perform these tasks.

The Business Requirement Assessment document contains columns that will help you to "MoSCoW" your requirements, so you can categorise them by priority.

I have also added a category, To Be Confirmed, (TBC.)

You can mark requirements as TBC if you're not yet ready (or able) to decide which MoSCoW queue they should be assigned to.

If you use TBC, set a review date to assign them to a MoSCoW category, so these items aren't forgotten!

High, Medium, or Low?

As an alternative to MoSCoW, the more simplistic HML or *high, medium* or *low* method can be used to prioritise, or rank items.

The main issue with HML is that this system is not very granular, especially when dealing with a large volume of potentially complex requirements.

You could consider a *Must* to be high priority, a *Should* to be medium priority, and a *Could* and *Won't* to be low priority, but you may still find a grey area where what is classed as high, or medium becomes heavily debated.

The beauty of MoSCoW is that the Must and Should categories allow us to acknowledge the high value of the tasks or requirements in both of these groups, but still allows them to be managed and considered separately.

However, HML does have its uses! In this book we will talk about scoring services, or specific functionality within the software that you are considering.

At this point, you may find it useful to associate "HML" with a numerical score out of 5, or 10.

So, for example, a high ranking item might have a score ranging from between 8-10, medium 5 to 7 and low, 1-4.

Project pitfall!
Watch out for "scope creep."

Once you've decided on your must have requirements, there is a risk that this list will keep expanding to include more and more items. This will make it harder to remain focused on what you *really* need when you begin reviewing software applications.
If keeping your "must" list small continues to be a challenge, try and imagine the worst that could happen if you choose NOT to pursue a requirement.

If the item truly helps you to achieve your goals, and your plans for your business will be compromised without it, then add it to your list.

This marks the end of chapter 2.

You now have the tools to put together a comprehensive, prioritised list of requirements to guide you when:

- Researching software products and watching product demonstrations
- Speaking with sales teams, software houses and consultancies

If you'd prefer to be guided through any of these processes, you can contact me here: hello@purposefulgroup.com

In chapters 3 and 4 we'll look at the relative merits of different types of software including cloud based apps, software as a service, enterprise software, desktop applications and the option to have your own bespoke software built.

References

Harvard Business Review. *Managing for Business Effectiveness.* https://hbr.org/1963/05/managing-for-business-effectiveness

Harvard Business Review. *Aligning Technology with Strategy.* https://hbr.org/product/harvard-business-review-on-aligning-technology-wit/an/10316-PDF-ENG

Toyota Traditions. *Ask 'why' five times about every matter.* http://www.toyota-global.com/company/toyota_traditions/quality/mar_apr_2006.html

CHAPTER 3

Why buy when you can rent? Licenses, SaaS, the Cloud, and your options

Over the next 2 chapters we'll review the pros and cons of different types of software, cloud based services and software hosting methods. The devil is in the detail, as they say, so we'll assess the various options in turn, including the common terminology used. (Unfortunately, there are so many names for the same products and services, that this often complicates the purchasing process.)

I'll suggest a number of ways to find good quality products in Chapter 7, but first let's review the types of software and services you're likely to encounter, and the implications of making one decision over another.

4 fundamental questions

It is common to see articles, blog posts and the like, which immediately launch into comparisons between different types of software, usually listing the advantages and disadvantages of SaaS (Software as a Service) vs. Enterprise software. Although these comparisons are useful, I believe that focussing on these points too soon is a mistake that misleads many businesses.

Initially, try to take a step back from this sort of information, and first look *inwards,* before looking *outwards.*

Your starting position should *always* be your specific characteristics, and requirements as a business, or department.

From this point, with a clear picture of what you need and why, you can follow a basic *process of elimination,* based on your business drivers and commercial needs.

Following this approach is far more likely to lead to a positive result.

As you review the information in this chapter, please keep the following questions in mind:

1. Do you wish to be able to "own" or adapt your software?

Do you want the freedom to use the software "for life," potentially holding it for as long as 3-10+ years? Is it important to have the scope to adapt it now, or in the future, or to be able to connect (i.e. *integrate*) it with other systems?

If you wish to extend, or flex a product to meet your needs, this is less likely to be possible with "rented" SaaS products, although moving up to a higher pricing tier *may* allow you to access a wider range of options.

On the other hand, "ownership" (via a license that allows you to modify the software, or the ability to hold it for a longer period) may *not* be the best option if:

- Your business is growing or changing quickly, and it might be better not to commit to a system for the long-term.
- You want to keep your options open. Better software is constantly coming onto the market via innovative vendors; many of them providing "free" software upgrades via the Software as a Service (SaaS) model.
- The cost of outright ownership is prohibitively expensive. (In chapter 5 we'll discuss the point at which leasing may become more expensive than owning your software!)

2. How urgently do you require the software?

If a short sales cycle is needed, consider that for larger and more complex software systems, it can take weeks (or even many months) to:

- Assess and gather together requirements
- Research the software available on the market
- Coordinate product demonstrations and trials
- Address outstanding questions
- Confirm details of financing
- Review contracts and terms
- Get staff trained up, and able to use the software correctly and to its fullest extent
- Carry out testing (user acceptance testing, UAT) to confirm that it supports your key business processes in the way(s) that you expect
- Install / implement the product and get it "set-up," including any

modifications to the software that you require. You may also need to factor in time to set up the hosting of the product and the transfer of data into the new system as part of your wider rollout plan.

In this case, "plug-and-play" cloud-based SaaS software that is hosted for you, or easy to install desktop products, will be much quicker to implement than self-hosted software, enterprise software that may require adjustments; usually referred to as customisation (code changes), or configuration (manual adjustments to fields, label names, menu options etc.) before you can use it, or bespoke software built for you from scratch. (We'll explore these options in some detail later in this chapter.)

3. Is convenience, or control most important?

- How critical is the software to the day-to-day running of your business?
- Are there legal, or regulatory requirements that you are bound to comply with?
- How severe would the consequences of non-compliance, hacking, or data theft be in terms of fines, loss of reputation, loss of business or compensation costs?
- What are your company's data security requirements?
- Do you have the in-house expertise to host the product yourself so you can control your security and data storage and backup arrangements, and manage compliance measures internally? Will you need to outsource the job and find 3rd party suppliers to manage hosting for you?

If you are looking to buy business critical-software and have lots of data protection or other regulations to consider, then *self-hosting* or *private cloud-based managed services* will give you more control than outsourcing to 3rd parties, or using SaaS based software.

However, if you are less concerned about these items, then SaaS products are generally more convenient, with fewer set-up tasks required.

4. Do you seek highly-specialised functionality?

How niche are your requirements?

If you are unable to find functionality that meets your needs on the open market, or you have masterminded a process or technique that you want your software systems to reflect, you may consider software that can be altered by a software provider, or decide to have a product built in-house, or by a 3rd party. (In the next chapter, we'll cover some key points to review if you are thinking of having software built, including options that could expedite the build of your product.)

The Public Cloud vs. The Private Cloud

"Gartner predicts that by 2019 that 30% of the 100 largest software vendors will have adopted a cloud-only model. More leading-edge IT capabilities will be available only in the cloud, forcing reluctant organizations closer to cloud adoption."

-Yefim Natis, Vice President and Gartner Fellow.

"The Cloud" is a generic, catch-all term. Cloud computing is simply a reliance on the Internet (supplied by a huge network of computers) for the storage and retrieval of data, services or software. Your *Intranet* services can also be serviced via the cloud.

Many types of cloud exist. These include:

- *Public clouds;* where resources (such as databases or servers) are shared with other customers of the service.
- *Private clouds;* where resources are *partitioned* to provide more security and privacy so that customers' data is kept ringfenced.
- *Hybrid clouds;* where services can be "mixed and matched" between shared and partitioned resources according to your requirements.
- *Named clouds,* marketed and owned by a particular organisation such as Microsoft Azure, AWS (Amazon Web Services) and IBM Cloud, and
- *Community clouds,* whereby resources and responsibilities are shared between several organisations.

We will focus on public and private clouds for the purposes of this book.

Let's look at their advantages and disadvantages.

Why choose software managed in the *private cloud*?	Why choose software managed in The *public cloud*?
The drivers – privacy, control, enhanced security and flexibility.	**The drivers - cost-effectiveness and convenience.**
Other terms associated with the private cloud: *"Single-tenant architecture"* and *"multi-instance architecture,"* *"partitioned hosting"*, *"dedicated hosting"*, *"private hosting."*	Other terms associated with the public cloud: *"Multi-tenant"* architecture, *shared hosting, public hosting. Software services delivered via the public cloud may be called on-demand software, hosted software, or Software as a Service (SaaS).*
The term "single-tenant" describes customers having exclusive access to their own copy of the software and a physically separate database and private infrastructure resources.	Where resources are shared with other businesses, data is *commingled*; meaning that customers share the *same* database and data is not kept physically separate.
To manage and control sensitive data. Enhance security, and compliance with regulations, such as DPA, HIPAA PCI DSS etc. by taking greater control over your data and where it is held. Compliance with regulations can be affected based on the location of the servers that hold your data – just one of many things that you will need to consider when selecting a supplier. (See Chapter 6 for more information about compliance and regulations.)	**Convenience.** Public cloud access and data storage typically come as part of the package when purchasing SaaS software. Minimal effort is required to get started.
To safeguard business critical software.	**Cost-effectiveness** is a benefit as resources are provided by the

Private resources may offer greater protection from threats and cyber-attacks as customers' data is kept physically separate in its own databases.

Flexibility. Self-hosted or private / multi-instance hosting services can often be configured, customised or re-arranged to meet your requirements.

The ability to scale usage and resources up, or down according to demand is an additional convenience that may be used to control costs.

Physical access to hardware and equipment. Depending on your arrangement with your cloud service provider (CSP), databases and other items may be accessible to authorised staff.

If this is the case, you may be free to troubleshoot some issues directly.

The negatives:

-Increased costs for cloud services which offer higher levels of security and privacy.

-Increased costs for customisation of services, (if required.)

software supplier and costs are shared between tenants.

The negatives:

-There is no direct access to your own data, unless this is via the software application.

-You must trust the vendor to maintain the service and take all reasonable precautions on your behalf.

-As a tenant, services are shared, and not private.

-Security is not as tight. Customers' data is *not* kept physically separate and all "tenants" are exposed to the same level of risk.

-You have no choice as to where

vendors' servers are held. Check terms and conditions to assess your compliance risk before forming a contract with a service provider – for example, where your business holds EU residents' data outside of the European Economic Area, (EEA).

Hosting and service options

When discussing cloud-based services, the term *hosting* often crops up.

Hosting is an activity which describes the way that the computing services you use are provided for you.

Hosting costs may be pay-as-you-go, or charged as a recurring fee based on the services consumed. There may also be up-front set-up costs, such as *provisioning fees* paid to the providers of the service to prepare hardware and other equipment and make it ready for use.

Cloud-based hosting options

In addition to deciding whether it is best to have your software and data *hosted* in the public, private or hybrid cloud, you will usually have 4 levels of service option. You may choose to:

1. Manage operations on site within your business, hosting the software yourself. This is what's known as the *self-hosting,* or *on-premises option.*
2. Rent a partially managed *colocation* service from a data centre.
3. Rent a fully hosted managed service from a *CSP (Cloud Service Provider.)*
4. Have your software and data completely managed for you by a provider of Software as a Service, (SaaS) or enterprise software as part of a packaged service available for a set period under the terms of a licensing agreement.

With the **self-hosting / on-premises model**, hosting is managed in your own building, or premises hence the terms *internal cloud,* or *on-premises* (often mistakenly referred to as *on-premise*, which has a completely different meaning and refers to a theory, or assumption.) The control and day-to-day responsibilities; including maintenance of your services and troubleshooting issues are yours, and you will need to have your own procedures in place, including disaster recovery plans and security policies, as well as the ability to meet the expense of buying, managing and maintaining your equipment.

You will need your own equipment if you are going to host a product yourself, so a person with the knowledge to obtain the right hardware, infrastructure and networking equipment to support your new software will be required. They will need to estimate the demand for the relevant tools and services both initially, and into the future, so the correct budget can be requested for your project, covering all the necessary items for some time to come, usually 2-5 years initially.

Accuracy is essential - an assessment which underestimates your requirements could cripple business activities and lead to disruption and issues with the day-to-day reliability of the software, such as system crashes and slow running software, whilst overestimates will result in unnecessary expense, wasted on equipment and services which are underutilised, or not required at all.

Other considerations include security measures such as putting firewalls (to protect your network and block unauthorised traffic) and anti-virus protection in place, plus other requirements such as compliance, storage space for equipment, bandwidth, database storage, backup, recovery and support. Depending on your software vendor, you may also need to take some responsibility for rolling out new software upgrades (improvements) and updates (such as bug fixes and code changes.)

If you are self-hosting, you will have a lot of decisions to make. These will include infrastructure and hardware equipment choices and suppliers, brands and costs. There will also be hiring decisions, should you need to employ staff to manage the infrastructure that supports your software.

Please note:
Software upgrades, updates, support and maintenance *may* still be chargeable and require collaboration between your software vendor and IT department.
You'll need to check how this works in each individual case. You will find some "clarification questions" that you can ask vendors and suppliers in Chapter 8.

Colocation is a variant of self-hosting. In this scenario, you would still own and maintain your equipment, hardware and software, do your own troubleshooting, and may also manage software upgrades or updates. However, the equipment is held at a type of *data centre (DC)* known as a *"colo"* or *colocation facility*, where space is rented and costs such as power and the general running of the facility are shared with other customers, whilst the control and segregation of your software and data is retained.

Any CSP, data centre, or colo centre should have *disaster recovery* plans in place to deal with *hacking, server crashes, fire, natural disasters, terrorism, power outages, damage to cables* and a host of other issues. Some data centres have the resources to run for several days in the event of a power cut!

The data centre *tier classification system* was set up to make it easier to compare the services offered by data centres around the world. *Tier 1* is the most basic and least resilient, whilst *Tier 4* data centres (the highest tier) include fault tolerance and other features that increase the data centre's resilience and minimise the impact of a range of possible failures on your IT services. You can find out more about the tier classification system here:
https://journal.uptimeinstitute.com/explaining-uptime-institutes-tier-classification-system/.

Some service companies and software vendors will have a *dual, or standby site*.

This is a second site where duplicate copies of their equipment are held; including databases, servers, hard drives and other key items. This is called *redundancy*, and processes are set up to *mirror*, or synchronise data storage at both sites. If redundancy is in place, there will also be a *failover* process which ensures that if services are lost at one location, they can be seamlessly switched over to the other site to provide continuity of service.

It is also worth knowing about a characteristic of data centres known as being *network*, or *carrier neutral*, which makes the service more flexible and convenient for customers. Using a carrier-neutral DC means that you are not tied-in to any particular providers, whether this relates to network providers, ISPs (Internet Service Providers) or other service providers when using the data centre. If a DC is *not* carrier-neutral, then you will have to go through the upheaval of changing data centres in order to change the companies that supply your services.

Fig 3 - Public and private cloud hosting options. Some options may be available in the public and private clouds. If data security and compliance are important, be sure to check how services are being hosted.

PUBLIC CLOUD	SELF-HOSTED (ON PREMISES, ON-PREM)	IS THERE A CASE FOR PAYING FOR "COLO" SERVICES RUN IN PUBLIC CLOUD?	**MANAGED SERVICES (HOSTED)**
PRIVATE CLOUD	SELF-HOSTED (ON PREMISES, ON-PREM)	COLOCATION, "COLO" CENTRE	**MANAGED SERVICES (HOSTED)**

(Left vertical arrow label: MOST SECURE / MOST CONTROL ... LEAST SECURE / LEAST CONTROL)

Managed / hosted cloud services. *CSPs, (Cloud Service Providers)* offer public and private cloud services and allow you to lease equipment and utilise their hardware and networking expertise, whilst maintaining a degree of security and control over your software and data.

Customers are therefore spared a large initial upfront investment.

With this option, all the moving parts and procedures (set-up, management, maintenance, troubleshooting etc.) are handled for you as part of the service package purchased. Services can usually be adjusted according to your requirements.

I cannot think of a reason why a business might pay for its own equipment and then pay for colocation services which sit in the *public cloud*, but for completeness, I have included this as a possible option.

Whether you require managed services, or wish to self-host, take a look at how a well-known managed cloud service businesses like *Rackspace* break down their costs and services: https://www.rackspace.com/en-gb/cloud/servers/pricing.

Please note:

There can be a lot of variation in terms of the services and standards that CSPs offer.

Some infrastructure may be shared between customers, whilst some may be available for private, rather than communal use.

Company standards and levels of security will also vary, so ask each company to lay-out their service model clearly so you know exactly what you will be getting.

A careful review of each company's Service Level Agreement (SLA) will help you identify the specific services on offer, as well as any limitations.

The private cloud's partitioned resources increase security, but there are arguments that the public cloud may have experienced so many hacks and attacks that these will only have fortified public cloud services, given the lessons learned because of these events.

Is the public cloud more secure for this reason?

The pros and cons of the public vs. private cloud outlined here are all relevant. Assess each service provider's policies and procedures and make an informed decision on a case-by-case basis.

Fig 4 - Inside a data centre. Credit. Global Access Point.

SaaS, PaaS, IaaS

Next, let's run through some other types of cloud-based services that you might come across.

Platform as a service (PaaS) is a type of cloud service that provides a platform for customers to develop, run, and manage applications without needing to build and maintain the infrastructure themselves. PaaS services, such as *Microsoft Azure* may be of interest to you if you are considering building your own software application.

Infrastructure as a Service (IaaS) is a type of cloud computing service that provides infrastructure resources such as hardware, networking and database storage over the Internet. One such provider, *Amazon Web Services, (AWS)* offers services to private individuals and businesses.

The 3rd type of cloud computing service is *Software as a Service (SaaS)*, which provides software services over the Internet. Let's begin our review of the advantages and disadvantages of SaaS, and other types of software product now.

Comparing different types of software

Off-the-shelf, commercial off-the-shelf (COTS), canned, packaged, or *shrink-*

wrapped software are all common names to describe commercial software that is built and ready-to-use (although, you might still require changes to be made to it.)

You're probably thinking that there are *too* many names for the same things. If so, I agree with you! However, keeping on top of the terminology discussed here will increase your confidence, and help you speak (and understand) the language of suppliers, so please stick with me.

We'll consider the pros and cons of buying bespoke software built exclusively for your business in the next chapter, but right now, let's review the merits and drawbacks of 3 different types of off-the-shelf product:

- Desktop software
- Enterprise software
- Software as a Service, (SaaS)

Why choose *Desktop Software*?

Key features:
- No reliance on web browsers (Internet Explorer, Google Chrome etc.) or Wi-Fi / network access to operate.
- Using the software outside of the office does not raise concerns about how to connect to it via a secure network.
- Assigning access to specific machines is straightforward.

The drivers:
Access can be assigned to specific PCs or laptops only.
Familiarity – as a traditional model, companies are used to this method of buying software.

Jargon associated with desktop software:
We are spared the jargon in the case of desktop software!
Aside from being generically referred to as "software", there aren't any other common names for it!
Data is stored locally on a laptop, PC or Mac and not in the cloud.
Data is not transmitted via the Internet.
You may consider this a benefit if you like the idea of data been stored *offline.*
You are free to choose a *best of breed* desktop product.

Specialist solutions are more likely to closely meet requirements than multi-purpose software. (We'll discuss best of breed software in chapter 7.)

Users of the software may have control over when downloads can take place, which reduces disruption and inconvenience.

Support and maintenance may be charged as extras, but are sometimes optional, rather than mandatory costs. (This should be confirmed.)

The negatives - Desktop Software

Desktop software is restrictive – it will only be available on PCs, Macs or laptops where the software has been installed.

Encryption may be needed. Laptops with the software installed may carry highly sensitive information. It may be necessary to encrypt laptops to protect data in the event of loss or theft.

Resource intensive desktop applications may use up more memory and processing power and lead to slow running laptops and PCs.

Manual software updates may be required, requiring effort from the user, although this may be minimal.

The restricted environment may complicate communication between staff. Because they are not connected to the web, desktop applications do not facilitate easy sharing of information. If the laptop or PC is Internet enabled, transferring data online or via email may then be possible.

Integration with other applications is difficult.

Data is stored locally on a laptop, PC or Mac and is *not* backed-up in the cloud. However, it is possible to buy back up software for desktop products. *IBM, Symantec, HP* and *Veritas* are some of the larger players able to back up software applications and data for you.

Risk of buying a product near the end of its life. Some argue that desktop products are dying out. Look for suppliers of desktop products with a large customer base, or decent market share and longevity in the market.

Reporting features can be limited, but may be more varied than those available in SaaS products.

Why choose *Enterprise Software*?

Description and key features:

- Larger scale software, generally offered with a choice of different software modules that customers can select from.
- Generally, one product is capable of serving *multiple* business functions.
- Enterprise software can usually be adapted – either manually, by making changes to the code, or both.
- Long term use of the software may be possible with the appropriate license.
- Superior reporting capabilities may be available
- Potential for integration with other products.
- Hosting options *may* be flexible.

The drivers:
Flexibility, choice, coverage across multiple business areas, integration capabilities.

Jargon associated with enterprise software:
Suite solution, enterprise system, enterprise solution, enterprise suite.
Ownership of the software, if purchased under a *perpetual license.*
(Be sure to confirm the licensing options available.)
We'll review different types of software licenses later in this chapter.
Customisation equals flexibility. Enterprise products can be tailored to meet your requirements. Customisation (code based changes) and configuration, (usually manual adjustments involving amendments to items such as the descriptions given to data entry fields, settings and menu options) are possible – usually with assistance from hired resources.
Users of the software may have control over when downloads can take place, which reduces disruption and inconvenience.
Integration with existing products. Having your enterprise product "talk to" or feed data between different systems is often possible as a built-in service, or billable extra.
Fewer applications are needed to run your business.
The software modules available in an enterprise application may not all be of the same standard. However, using enterprise software may allow you to serve multiple business functions by picking the "modules" that meet your needs.
User access and *permissions management* tools may be available to

control the data that staff can view, update, print, create and delete – important when meeting compliance requirements such as *HIPAA, The Data Protection Act,* the forthcoming *GDPR* and in the prevention of fraud and data theft. See Chapter 6 for more about these laws and regulations.

Reporting is usually available and customisable to suit your business needs.

Cross-platform-friendly. Web based applications can be used via any mobile device, PC, Mac or laptop with a web browser installed and Wi-Fi access.

You may have a choice of hosting options and may be able to:
i) Have the software hosted for you by the software provider (so it behaves as a SaaS product)
ii) Host it yourself in-house, (self-hosting)
iii) Outsource the hosting service to a cloud service, or colo provider, or
iv) Use a desktop version of an enterprise product

The negatives - Enterprise Software

Flexibility comes at a price. Complexity and costs may increase when customising / configuring software. This work may be charged to you at an hourly or daily rate. Excessive customisation, add-ons and extras can quickly drain financial resources. Rather than ploughing thousands of pounds or dollars into changes, you may wish to seek out a product that is a better fit.

The amount of software provided may be "overkill." Enterprise software may provide more functionality than is necessary. If you only require one module from a suite, it may make better financial sense to buy a single product instead.

Long-term tie-in. You may feel obligated to keep software long-term due to its expense, possibly causing you to miss out on the latest advances in software and technology.

The range of software "modules" provided across business functions may be of variable quality with a mixed bag of high-performance best of breed offerings along with modules of a lower standard.

Complex to implement...and to "rip out". Software that is fully integrated with a range of in-house systems will be more difficult to rip out and replace in future.

More complex to learn and operate. More time for training / learning may be required for larger software applications.

Enterprise software is not always as flexible as you might expect. Beware of the "tail wagging the dog" - inflexible systems which impose unwelcome limitations such as fixed sets of billing cycles or reporting periods. Check that products are *truly* flexible enough to meet your needs and *don't* force you to follow processes that are not right for your company.

Enterprise licenses can be an expensive up front cost, tying-up business capital. They are generally classed as a capital expense rather than an operating expense.

Expect a longer time for achieving ROI*/TTV** due to the cost, complexity and set-up time to configure / customise the software before it can be used.

Hosting may be managed separately and charged as a separate expense depending on the type of enterprise software purchased and whose services you use to host the software. As a result, a business may have multiple contracts and agreements to manage.

Why choose Software as a Service, (SaaS)?

Description and key features:

- SaaS is leased software supplied via the Internet – usually, via the public cloud.
- Maintenance, upgrades, updates, bug fixes and data storage are all managed for you, usually rolled into one recurring subscription package paid for on a monthly, quarterly or annual basis.
- SaaS products are offered on a temporary license that normally lasts for the duration of each paid subscription period.
- Resources and infrastructure are provided on a "multi-tenant" basis, meaning that software, hardware, database storage and other services are shared between customers with no physical partitioning of data. This makes SaaS cost effective, but possibly less secure than private cloud based solutions.

The drivers:
Cost effectiveness, convenience simplicity, innovation.

Jargon associated with SaaS:
"On-demand software", cloud computing, cloud-based software, hosted software, multi-tenant software, rented software, leased software.
Quick start and quick time to value, TTV.
TTV is the time taken to derive benefit from your software.
With SaaS, there is nothing to install or download.
(However, data may still need to be loaded into the system and basic configuration, set-up and staff training may still be required.)
You are free to choose a *best of breed* SaaS product.
Specialist solutions created for a specific purpose are more likely to clos requirements than generic, multi-purpose software.
(We'll revisit the concept of *best of breed software* in Chapter 7.)
Maintenance, upgrades, equipment and support are generally taken care of for you under an all-inclusive subscription fee with no need for extra resources, or staff. Services such as automatic upgrades (delivery of enhanced versions of the software), hosting, hardware and equipment, data storage, support and backups are included and there are no charges to update software.
This is ideal for those with small IT departments, without the in-house expertise to host the product internally, or to manage more complex arrangements.
Cashflow-friendly pricing model. Subscription based costs are usually classed as operating (rather than capital) expenses.
There is no large upfront charge. Budgeting is simpler when pricing is based on an all-inclusive model.
Highly flexible / scalable arrangement. With a SaaS product, you are not tied-in to one particular version of the product.
As a rule, by selecting a cheaper, or more expensive subscription package you may increase or decrease the functionality, or level of service received.
Innovative and modern. It may be fair to say that SaaS vendors work harder to innovate and continuously improve their products.
Many keep pace with customers' requests and other commercial trends, knowing that this will maintain customer loyalty and lead to subscription renewals. This is essential for maintaining a consistent level of income as there is no upfront license fee for them to rely on. SaaS products *may* also have a more modern design than traditional software products.

Relatively easy to cancel contract and switch suppliers at short notice. Contracts may only require 1 months' notice for cancellation. (Check terms and conditions to be certain.) Limited integration capabilities mean that the software is also easier to "rip-out" and replace.

Cross-platform-friendly. Please see the comments under the same heading for Enterprise Software.

SaaS vendors may reward loyalty. Instead of paying month-to month you may be able to pay for 3, 6, or 12 months in advance at a discount, reducing costs further. (You may wish to pay month-to-month for a while to trial the product first before you commit to a longer term!)

Many SaaS providers offer *freemium* products which are free forever, or until a threshold is reached. This could save you money if the free option is suitable for you. It will also allow you to "try before you buy."

One single contract for software and hosting, keeps paperwork and agreements simple.

The negatives - Software as a Service

The trade-off for cost-effectiveness is sharing - shared data storage, shared resources...and shared risks.

Ownership costs may surpass those for enterprise software beyond the 2-5 year+ mark. Extrapolate several years ahead to calculate the most economical option over several years. We'll review software costs in more detail in Chapter 5.

Integration between different products is difficult, or even impossible.

An Internet connection and access to a web browser is needed to access the software.

A loss of Internet / network access may affect staff's productivity.

Costs are not fixed. The supplier is free to raise their subscription charges at any time, as per their terms of business.

Fees based on usage limits can escalate. Costs will rise if usage, data storage thresholds or higher user numbers push your business into a higher, less economical pricing tier.

Support is not *always* included. Some SaaS companies charge extra for telephone or email based support. Some only provide online FAQs, videos, PDFs or community support for free.

Failure to pay the subscription fee will result in revoked access to the

software, and your data until your account is settled. Your data is being managed for you and without access to the software, there is no access to the data you put into it!

Lack of control. You will have no control over when updates take place and limited / no ability to make changes to the software. You will be 100% reliant on your vendor and their support, security and data management protocols and processes. No access to code or infrastructure will be permitted and customisation is not possible. Standard contracts and terms are generally offered to all customers on a "take it or leave it" basis.

Security concerns away from the office. To maintain security off-site, measures may need to be put in place to provide secure network access, such as VPNs (virtual private networks.)

Reporting features can be limited, if available.

Limited features for managing user permissions. User permissions may be very simple, or may not exist at all.

*ROI - Return on Investment.
**TTV - Time to Value.

Please note:

- Make sure that any parts of a product that *can't* be changed are *fully understood and accepted* by your business.

- Some desktop applications have cloud based alternatives, whilst some enterprise software is available in desktop format, or in the cloud. They are discussed as separate entities here to highlight the distinctions between them.

  It is important to be aware that the <u>same product</u> may have *different* pros, cons and characteristics in its desktop, or cloud-based forms. Cloud versions of software may offer *less* functionality, but more convenience. Weigh up the pros and cons using the information provided above.

  Of course, some vendors have mobile apps too. These are important to consider, but are not covered in the tables because mobile apps do not usually *drive* software purchasing decisions - although the quality of a vendor's app may influence your purchasing decision.

- Some software suppliers offer hosted software services via the private cloud. Ask whether this is possible if this service interests you - it never does any harm to ask! Weigh up the pros and cons before deciding - the downsides to this arrangement are complexity, and possibly cost. If the company the software is purchased from and the 3rd party hosting company are different, you will have two sets of contracts to manage and two sets of fees payable to each company. Bear in mind that if any issues arise, you may need to coordinate between multiple companies.

- *The tables cover standard inclusions and exclusions, but there will be exceptions to the rule and software services will continue to evolve. As an example, you may have noticed that it is now possible to connect to the* <u>Internet</u> *via the* <u>desktop</u> *version of Microsoft Office!*

Never assume that benefits come as standard and confirm all features, functionality and services on a per product basis to avoid misunderstandings.

Software licensing

It is strongly recommended that you check the type of license being offered to you, along with the terms laid out in the software licensing agreement before making a commitment.

Most licenses will include clauses confirming the duration of the license, who may use it and what it may be used for:

- **Perpetual licenses** never expire and run on indefinitely.
- **Annual licenses** require renewal and further payments once the current license has expired.
- **Non-perpetual licenses / subscription licenses** are time limited, and usually tied to a recurring payment where software is "leased" for a period. Access is revoked (or software is deactivated, or must be uninstalled) if the license is not renewed.

Proprietary software licenses
You may also come across the term, *proprietary software license.*

These licenses allow the individual or company that created the software to retain ownership of it, whilst permitting copies of the software to be used in accordance with a contract, commonly known as an *end-user license agreement,* or *EULA.*

EULAs establish an agreement between anyone who downloads, installs or purchases software and the developer of the software, and may apply to all types of software from desktop and web based products, to mobile apps.

Not all EULAs require paperwork to be signed. Often, the user agrees to be bound by the terms of the developer's EULA just by using an application, even if no written contract exists. In other cases, the user must agree to the terms before the software can be accessed. All rights are reserved by the developer, and the *source code*; (the set of human-readable instructions and commands which form the basis of the software) is retained as the Intellectual Property of the developer.

EULAs and restrictions

EULAs may impose a number of restrictions, or limits on users. Limitations to be aware of include:

- **The number of licenses available to you** under a *volume, or per seat license. Capped* or *usage based restrictions* may require additional fees to be paid if limits are exceeded. For example, you may have 50 licenses, but if you require 51 or more, you will need to pay extra for them.

- **The use of licenses assigned to a named person, or PC** (called *named user licenses, named PC, or named workstation licenses.* They may also be called *single user* or *individual licenses).* For example, PC-1056 and PC-1078 may be licensed to run the software purchased. Anyone wishing to use the software would therefore need to use either of these machines.

- **Distribution restrictions.** Leasing, sublicensing, giving, or lending of the software are generally prohibited.

- **Caps on the maximum number of users who can access the software *at the same time***, if you have a *concurrent license.* For example, rather than buying 50 licenses, you may estimate that only 30 staff are likely to need the software *at exactly the same time* and decide to buy a license that will allow 30 simultaneous users. Once the limit of 30 users is reached, user 31 will be unable to access the software.

- **Software that is available to users at a particular site, or business only**, known as a *site license or enterprise license.* It may be called an *unlimited site license* if user numbers are unrestricted.

Licenses may, or may not include support, upgrades and maintenance as part of the license fee.

This is where vendors make their money, so these are often chargeable extras, especially in the case of desktop and enterprise software!

Open source software licenses

If you intend to have software built for you, then you may wish to get a head start using *Open Source Software (OSS)*. The source code for open source software is made available publicly using an *open source license.*

If researched carefully, using OSS may be a faster, cheaper option than paying for developers to create similar functionality from scratch. Developers will be working with a shell, or even a fairly well-developed product that can be used to speed up delivery of your project.

A word of warning: avoid the temptation to try and wrestle a product into meeting your needs.

If the product is not a good fit, it may be cheaper to select another product which is a better match and will require less work to adapt, or to build one from scratch.

There are many licenses associated with open source software, including the popular *Apache, MIT* and *GNU GPL (GNU General Public License)*. Most are available free of charge, but this should be confirmed per license.

OSS license holders usually have the right to change the source code, and distribute the software for commercial or private purposes free of charge, but it is important to apply for the appropriate license and understand its terms of use and restrictions.

Terms and conditions are usually available from the website that the source code was downloaded from, or from the software licensor's website.

Note that the terms of your open source license *may* state that the code produced must be made public, so it is important to look out for any restrictions that will apply to you, or affect your ability to maintain your competitive advantage.

You can find more information about OSS, and OSS licenses here:

https://opensource.org/

https://opensource.org/licenses/category

http://www.openforumeurope.org/

https://www.apache.org/licenses/LICENSE-2.0

https://www.gnu.org/licenses/gpl-3.0.en.html

https://opensource.org/licenses/mit-license.php

Finding Open Source projects

There are plenty of open source business applications, including CRM (Customer Relationship Management), CMS (Content Management System) and BI (Business Intelligence) software.

To find suitable Open Source projects you can Google: *open source* + [*the type of software that interests you.*] E.g. *open source CRM.*

You can also use websites popular within the development community to find them, including:

Github, the world's biggest platform for developers: https://github.com/explore.

Sourceforge, another well-established site: https://sourceforge.net/.

Open source as alternative: https://www.osalt.com.

Please note:
The source code for open source software is publicly available - this means that in theory hackers can study the code for vulnerabilities and security loopholes that they can exploit. However, some argue that open source products are more secure; so many programmers work on the code, that they believe that flaws are more likely to be spotted and addressed.

If you would like to know more about what might be involved in building software rather than buying or leasing it, then there is more information provided in the next chapter.

If not, please join me in Chapter 5, where we'll look at the *true cost* of purchasing your software.

References

Gartner. *Gartner Says By 2020, a Corporate "No-Cloud" Policy Will Be as Rare as a "No Internet" Policy Is Today*. http://www.gartner.com/newsroom/id/3354117.

The Uptime Institute describes itself as "an unbiased advisory organisation focused on improving the performance, efficiency, and reliability of business-critical infrastructure."

The Uptime Institute: *Data centre tier classification system*. https://uptimeinstitute.com/tiers, https://journal.uptimeinstitute.com/explaining-uptime-institutes-tier-classification-system/.

Uptime Institute Global Tier Certification Map. https://uptimeinstitute.com/TierCertification/certMaps.php.

CHAPTER 4

Made-to-measure: Buying, or building bespoke software

This chapter is exclusively about bespoke software development.

If you'd like to find out more about what's involved in building, or having software built for you; including the benefits, pitfalls and challenges, you'll find useful information here. Otherwise, please skip to the next chapter!

Many of the clients that I have worked for have bought software under a license and paid to have it customised, but have later made the decision to develop their own software "in house."

You may be considering building a team or augmenting an existing IT department with the skills needed to build a software product from scratch. Alternatively, you may be thinking about outsourcing the work to a company that can build a bespoke product for you. This may be a suitable option, if you:

- Have very specific requirements, whether these relate to your industry sector, internal processes, or particular integrations that you want in place between your new software and other in-house systems.
- Cannot find software on the market to meet your needs.
- Choose not to compromise with features or processes that are not exactly as you'd like them.
- Have identified functionality (which is not available elsewhere) that would give your company a competitive advantage.
- Wish to have complete control (and lifetime ownership) of your software.
- Have a mature IT department (or the funds to hire in temporary

expertise) and do not want, or need to deal with software vendors, or the process of purchasing off-the-shelf products.

- Have an ongoing internal demand for new software and tools which can be modified and extended "at will."

Let's consider some of the main advantages and disadvantages.

Why develop bespoke software in-house?	Why outsource development to a 3rd party?
Key features: Software is built by your own employees, or freelancers hired to work for you from home, or at your place of business. Jargon associated with bespoke software builds: *proprietary software, in-house development, custom build*, custom development*, bespoke software*, bespoke development*, tailor-made software*.* **The drivers** Complete control, flexibility and choice.	**Key features:** Software is built by a 3rd party consultancy or software house. Jargon associated with bespoke software builds: *See all the items to the left marked with an asterisk, *. The software will only be proprietary if you own the rights to it.* **The drivers** Control, flexibility and choice, with responsibility for building the product sitting with a 3rd party.
Advantages - No license fees. - No support, or maintenance fees to pay to 3rd parties. These costs do not disappear, but now you will be able to manage them yourself! - Total ownership of source code, and of a unique product. - Competitive advantage. - Full control over the product's	**Advantages** - No license fees.** - Total ownership of source code, and of a unique product.*** - Competitive advantage.*** - Full control over the product's features and its evolution over time.** - The possibility of agreeing a fixed price for the software to

features and its evolution.
- No reliance on 3rd parties to develop software.

Disadvantages
- You will bear the responsibility for hiring and managing staff; developers, testers, business analysts, a project manager, software support staff, plus hardware, networking and infrastructure specialists if you decide to do the build work yourself.
- With an internal build, costs are harder to fix, and will escalate if the project overruns, or if more people are brought onto the project.
- If your team is inexperienced there is some risk that the venture may not go according to plan.

Common disadvantages for in-house and 3rd party projects
- Can be expensive. The cost / benefit balance should be considered carefully. Are there off-the-shelf products that might serve your needs at a lower cost and without the wait-time associated with a bespoke build?
- You will need to factor in ongoing costs for hosting, whether you go down the self-hosting, managed hosting or *colo* route.
- There will be additional costs for

be built.
- Requirements are handed off to a 3rd party who take on the responsibility of creating and delivering the product.

Disadvantages
- Product maintenance and support of the software, including upgrades, updates and other changes will tie you to a supplier (either the original supplier, or another supplier) for the life of the product, unless your business has the resources to take over these tasks.
- Having software built from scratch by a 3rd party is arguably riskier than buying an existing product. (Another very good reason to request frequent updates, *visibility* of progress and to make staged payments based on progress.)
- Training documents will have to be created from scratch. The company providing the software is likely to charge extra for this.

The disadvantages to the left, labelled: *Common disadvantages for in-house and 3rd party projects* also apply.

networking and hardware equipment if you intend to host the software yourself, or use a *colo* service.
- Most existing products will probably have some form of training or support documentation. With a new product, this will all have to be created from scratch.

**Always confirm the exact rules of engagement with the consultancy / software house before proceeding and have these in writing.
***Bespoke software will offer few benefits if you agree to unfavourable terms!
In Chapter 9, we'll review some important legal considerations to keep in mind when reviewing contracts and negotiating terms.

Building your own software

Having seen many projects from idea through to launch for clients, my top tips for building software in house are:

Allow more time and money than you think you'll need for any bespoke software project managed in-house. Development projects can be complex and resource intensive with many moving parts. It is notoriously difficult to estimate delivery dates accurately. This is project management territory, but you *are* managing a project, so a plan is needed, along with contingencies to cover worst-case scenarios.

If you need to recruit a team allow enough time to find staff with the right skills and experience. Good tech staff are often expensive and may be earning high salaries as permanent workers, or will be freelancing; usually charging clients on a day-rate. Even if you intend to hire an employment agency to find staff, allow at least 4 weeks to get to the stage of issuing employment contracts, plus an additional 4 to 6 weeks in case your new hires have notice periods to work before they can join you.

If you cannot pay market rates, or are based outside of a major city centre, then factor in further time to complete the hiring process - unless you will permit staff to work part-time, or from home, which will make the job more attractive, but will require you to manage staff remotely. Chapter 11 contains links to some project and team management tools that are useful for coordinating and managing teams working on-site (co-located teams), or off-site (distributed teams.)

Attempt to derisk the process by building the product in small parts and *always* build your "must haves" first. (See Chapter 1 for a recap on using the MoSCoW prioritisation process.) Breaking down the product into the essentials may allow you to build some small-scale, but valuable functionality or "widgets" before exiting gracefully with something to show for your efforts if things don't work out as expected.

The approach of building the product in *iterations*, or *increments* over time can work very well as a software development strategy. Making systematic improvement and small, regular releases of functionality are some of the principle tenets of *Agile software development,* which we'll discuss shortly.

Consider using open source software (OSS) and plug-ins to speed up development
We talked about *OSS* in Chapter 3. Software can also be extended via *plug-ins*; widgets, or components that can be bolted-on to an existing product to enhance it, or to extend it by adding completely new functionality. Experienced developers should be able to carry out research to find OSS and plug-ins that i) meet your needs, ii) are stable and reliable and iii) can be worked on using a programming language that they are proficient in.

Once you start, you'll face demands to keep developing the software
Aside from maintenance and bug fixes, expect new requirements and requests to come from staff. You will find that issues, and opportunities for improvement will be identified as staff use the software, and as a result of your business growing, or evolving.

Adding more people to development projects doesn't necessarily make the process "go faster." This is a common misconception. In the same way that you wouldn't expect to hire workmen to replace the carpet in your bedroom and paint the room at exactly the same time, there are certain development tasks that must run *sequentially*, rather than in *parallel*.

At these times, no matter how large a team you have, certain tasks will have to be completed before others can begin.

Fig 5 - Parallel and sequential tasks.

Three tasks run in *parallel*. Tasks1, 2 and 3 can all be coded at the same time.

Three tasks run in *sequence*. Task 1 must be completed before task 2 can start and tasks 1 & 2 must be completed before task 3 can start.

The other important thing to remember is that new members of staff are often a drain on a team initially and take time to become productive.

When existing staff train new people, this will slow down development, not speed it up! Therefore, a plan for extra staff must be factored in far enough in advance for new staff to be able to contribute in helping you hit your deadline. Doing this too late, or as a cure-all for a delayed project will only make the situation worse.

Forming a team

When building a product in-house you will need to consider everything you would normally entrust a supplier to take care of for you. This list will give you some idea of where your money goes when buying software!
You may need to hire competent individuals with the following skills:

- *Developers* (full-time or freelance) - to build the product and make it available to your staff. They will need to maintain the software, fix bugs and release software updates or patches (code used to update systems to fix bugs and to make security, software or hardware related adjustments), back up data and manage your databases (a job also done by a *DBA, Database Administrator*) and release upgrades; or new and improved versions of the software. Developers may also help you connect, or integrate different software products so that information can be transferred between them.
  Developers often specialise in one or two programming languages and are typically described as being *front-end, back-end* or *full-stack* developers.

  Front-end (or *client-side*) skills are used to create the parts of apps that a user can see and interact with. Front-end developers usually control elements of a software application such as the layout, fonts, styling, menu options and buttons. Common examples of front-end skills include: CSS (Cascading Style Sheets), JavaScript, jQuery and HTML, (Hyper Text Markup Language).

Back-end (or *server-side*) skills are used to perform actions which take place at the "back-end", also known as the database. A back-end developer's work might include capturing the information entered into a software application and storing it in a database, and the retrieval and presentation of that data on-screen at a later date. Back-end developers are usually skilled in a programming language; PHP, Python, Ruby or Java for example, combined with solid database experience.

Full-stack developers are multi-skilled developers, experienced and competent in both front and back-end technologies. However, it is challenging to maintain such a broad-skillset, especially as technology moves at such a fast pace.

- *DevOps,* is a portmanteau of the words *development* and *operations*. These specialists bring together these two disciplines to automate processes that help development teams manage and release software.
- *Infrastructure / network engineers* – to maintain, monitor and upgrade your network services and hardware equipment.
- *An IT manager or development manager* - to manage the team (or a senior developer able to write code and manage the team).
- *Technical / product support staff* - once the product is built, you will need to commit to supporting it. Support staff will troubleshoot, respond to queries and resolve issues raised by software users.
- *Software testers* - act as the guardians of software quality, testing the product for bugs and issues and highlighting problems to the development team.
- *Security* experts - advise on, and implement security best-practice, putting protocols in place to protect businesses from internal and external security threats.
- *Technical architects* - plan and influence everything from the approach taken to build the software, any integration with other products that is required and how this will be achieved, management and storage of data and even the programming

language to be used for the project. A lack of foresight, or failure to consider the big-picture could make development work more complex or problematic both initially, and in the future.

- *User experience (UX)* - this involves looking at the layout of elements on screen, the processes and activities that the software needs to support, consistency and flow when using the product and ensures that the user interface is logical and enjoyable to use. Would you agree that an easy-to-use system that people like working with might encourage productivity?

- *Designers* - are concerned with the visuals and "look and feel" of the product.
  Note that conflicts between design "form" and development "function" happen frequently.
  It is possible that designs can look amazing, but be challenging, or even impossible to implement, because the design does not take important practical or technical considerations into account. Before falling in love with a design, check that it can be translated into software by a developer!

- *A project manager* - to manage, monitor and coordinate the team's activities and to report on project progress.

- *Business analysts (BAs)* - to research, organise, and manage the requirements for the product, and help your business achieve consensus about what will be done. They may conduct feasibility studies and present cost estimates to management for review. BAs often map out and document existing and planned business processes, ensuring that the vision and wishes of your business are understood and correctly translated into working software by the development team.

- *Trainers* - will be needed later in the project to make sure that staff understand how to use the product and get the best from it. Whoever delivers the training should understand the product well, understand the way(s) in which your staff will use it, and have the necessary interpersonal and communication skills to deliver quality training sessions.

- *Content / copy writers* - prepare the text that exists within your software application including error messages, entry field labels and help text. They may also write Frequently Asked Questions (FAQs) and support manuals for your staff to refer to. (Trainers, business analysts, or your own staff may also be able to help with this - in fact, using familiar company jargon throughout your app will make it easier for staff to learn how to use it!)

Other things to consider...
- *Software*. Whilst building, and supporting your product your tech team will use a range of software, including; tools to help them with testing the software, analysing and monitoring the "health" of the product, "housing" and maintaining the code that has been written, and maintaining and supporting the product from a hardware or software perspective. If you have a team of developers, there are also developer (or programmer) licenses to arrange before they can write code in your language of choice, tools used to manage the release of software and to introduce safeguards so that the team does not overwrite each other's work and tools to manage different versions of the software.

  Support staff will usually organise their queries using help desk or customer service tools for logging feedback and issues raised by staff and business analysts and project managers may use software for creating charts and diagrams and project tracking.

  Experienced staff will know what software they need, but of course, they will be expecting you to pay for it!
- *Hosting and infrastructure related costs.* You will have costs for hardware, software and networking equipment, bandwidth, servers, databases and database storage (usually in the magnitude of gigabytes (GB) or terabytes (TB) - the equivalent of 1,024 gigabytes), equipment storage costs and power costs. We'll talk more about the general costs associated with buying software in the next chapter.

If you outsource the build of the software, but the company building it will *not* be hosting it for you, you might ask them if they can recommend any colocation, or managed cloud services.
We'll discuss due diligence checks for products and suppliers in Chapters 7-9.

Make sure you understand what makes technical staff "tick."

I have seen small organisations assign multiple roles to staff to save money and manage head count.

This can work, but it is important to be aware of the pitfalls of this approach.

Coding requires deep concentration, and many developers prefer to code exclusively. Some may feel overloaded, or demotivated by time distributed across other tasks.

This can lead to staff retention issues, as developers leave to find jobs where they can focus on using and developing their specialist skills.

It is time consuming to find skilled staff, and you may even have paid a finder's fee for them. Therefore, it makes little sense to drive them away by creating a working environment not suited to technically minded folks.

Consider the time and money to replace staff members before implementing processes that may prove to be unpopular.

If you want staff to use a range of skills on a regular basis, actively search for and create a tech team who are stimulated by variety and are not necessarily looking to become experts as their career progresses.

Bear in mind that if staff are doing a range of tasks, then a lack of focus can become an issue. In the case of developers with hybrid roles, this will slow the rate of development and possibly affect product quality - even if they are happy to multi-task. It is also important to consider that people with a breadth of skills may not always have the expertise of a specialist.

Things to consider when outsourcing software development work

If you decide to outsource the build of your software to a 3rd party:

- **Beware of companies that say they will take your requirements and come back to you with the finished product** *without* further consultation. Reaching a shared vision can be tricky, and software developed in silos can disappoint. For best results, an approach where the product is developed in a transparent manner and progress is regularly demonstrated, is a good idea. Be prepared to answer questions and to be involved in the process. Always request that consultancies provide diagrams, process flow documents, wireframes (a basic skeleton of the system), and designs you can review to reduce the risk of misunderstandings arising.

- **A financial agreement based on staged payments as the project successfully reaches agreed milestones,** is probably the safest way to proceed.
- **Note that the lead time** will vary according to your requirements, but could be anything between a few weeks to many months.
- **Companies you intend to review your plans with should sign an NDA** before discussions commence. NDAs (non-disclosure agreements) are discussed in Chapter 9 along with other matters relating to contracts and agreements.
- **Make sure that you will own the intellectual property rights (IPR) to the software and source code** and are free to do as you wish with it, including being at liberty to use it in perpetuity and allowing other companies to manage it for you.
- **Do your due diligence checks**, including asking if you can take up references from past customers. Sample questions for reference calls and visits are included in Chapter 9.

What is Agile software development?

I became a certified Scrum master (CSM) in 2008 and have used a range of Agile development approaches including SCRUM, XP, and SCRUMban. Having coached and trained both technical and non-technical teams new to Agile development, I know this way of working can seem a little strange!

Organisations such as *Google, Spotify, Amazon* and *Microsoft* have all used Agile in its various forms, and many software consultancies now use Agile development techniques. You may even be considering following Agile practices in-house.

Therefore, in this section you will find information about some of the Agile principles and practices that you may come across.

Agile teams believe in:

- *Focusing on delivering value for customers,*
- *Seeking feedback, making incremental improvements and taking time to reflect on what works and what doesn't,*
- *Controlling the duration of tasks and activities to maximise focus and output (reducing the effect of Parkinson's Law, whereby "work expands to fill the time available for its completion"!),*
- *Maintaining open team and stakeholder communication and,*
- *Keeping things simple, to deliver value and increase customer satisfaction.*

Agile is actually an umbrella term, the Agile family includes *XP (eXtreme Programming), Scrum, Kanban, Lean* and *DSDM (Dynamic Systems Development Method) frameworks.*

It is usually contrasted with Waterfall, a more traditional software development methodology.

Agile frameworks emerged from a desire to overcome some of the issues known to plague "traditional" software development projects and the Agile mindset reflects a more pragmatic approach to building software.

There is an acceptance that we will always have the *least* amount of knowledge at the start of a project and there is an appreciation that a customer's requirements may evolve as a project progresses.

Agilists believe in making frequent releases of software and the mantra "release early, release often" in order to obtain feedback and make improvements, is well-known.

Agile allows change to be managed flexibly *and* efficiently, by **breaking tasks down, prioritising ruthlessly, and releasing software in recurring development cycles** called sprints, or *iterations* (meaning "to repeat"), which may last anything from a week to 30 days before they end, and begin again.

Agile development teams add functionality to products *incrementally* over time, *iterating over* the work done to enhance, or extend the software.

This contrasts with the *"big bang"* style of release associated with Waterfall, where a large amount of functionality, usually built over a longer time period is delivered all at once.

I think of the Waterfall methodology as being like a relay race, with the baton (the software), being passed between different stages and teams. The team crosses the finish line just once during the project, with those whose tasks come towards the end of the race coming under pressure to make up any time lost by those who completed their work at an earlier stage! Usually it is the testing phase that faces the squeeze. *This phase is critical to having a high-quality, bug-free product and yet, when following the Waterfall methodology, it is often denied the attention that it deserves.*

In contrast, in Agile teams, professionals with a mix of different technical skills work together and operate as a single unit. This encourages better teamwork and ownership of the entire project, and not just an interest in *"my* part" vs. *"your* part" of the project. Testing is carried out *throughout* the project, rather than at the end, so there is no last-minute rush to check that features are working correctly. In conjunction with better quality, and more frequent communication with customers, this also reduces the risk that a company will disappear for months, and then reappear with a substandard product.

When Agile is executed well, in other words, not quasi-Agile or "Wagile", (the often unfortunate product of a combined Waterfall-Agile approach) and teams understand what they are doing and *why*, it is extremely powerful. Each member of the Agile family has its own set of practices.

Scrum's repeating development cycles are called *sprints.* At the start of each sprint, a *sprint goal* is set, which describes the working software and tasks that the development team intends to deliver during the sprint. The work is pulled from a product to-do list called a *product backlog.* This list includes a prioritised set of requirements, features, enhancements, technical tasks, and bugs and *user stories* (small, self-contained units, or "building blocks" of functionality), which when added together result in a larger body of functionality, or a product. The order of items can be changed and work can be prioritised, or deprioritised.

At the end of the sprint cycle, the team demonstrates the completed work to the customer, reflect on the highs and lows experienced during the sprint and brainstorms ways to make improvements for the next one.

XP (short for eXtreme Programming), is known for the practice of *pair programming.* This involves two developers working on a single task on a *shared computer,* writing code and solving problems together.) "Two heads are better than one," as the proverb goes! Followers of XP believe that together, developers will come up with better solutions than they would do alone and that quality will increase as the paired developers pick up on each other's mistakes. XP also has iterations (not sprints), which usually last 1 or 2 weeks.

Lean and *Kanban* (which means "sign" or "card" in Japanese) emerged from the manufacturing sector and places an emphasis on customer value, efficiency and eliminating waste.

The Software Development Life Cycle (SDLC)

The Software development process is a cycle. Whether you build, or buy your product, every one of them will have gone through these stages, to a greater, or lesser extent!
The basic elements of the cycle may vary slightly in terms of terminology and where the cycle "officially" starts and ends, but overall the cycle is the same. Agile development rapidly passes through all the stages of the cycle in a single *sprint,* or *iteration*, whilst a Waterfall project moves through the stages of the cycle just once, in order, cascading down like a waterfall, (hence the name) until the project is completed.
It can be useful to understand what the stages of the life cycle are. Here's an example:

Concept. This stage includes the birth of the initial idea, the exploratory work needed to decide whether the idea should be pursued and the development of the idea through research and data analysis. (Some also call this the *Discovery phase*.)

Requirements gathering and analysis includes taking the initial concept and producing a set of *requirements* (the description of what the users of the software will need to be able to do, as well as the technical tasks that must be actioned if the software is to run reliably.) This stage involves mapping out the steps and processes involved in helping users get from "A to B" using your product, (sometimes called *user journeys*), and how the system will need to behave in different scenarios.

Design (not to be confused with *visual design*) looks at how the system needs to be *architected* in order to fulfil the requirements. It takes the components of the system; their structure and organisation and the flow of data within it into consideration. It also considers the hardware to support the product and the programming language(s) that might be used to build the product.

Strangely, the SDLC does not explicitly mention the user experience (UX) and visual design elements of the process that are concerned with the ease-of-use of the product, the layout of elements on screen, colour schemes and the "look and feel" of the product. I've referenced them here because they should not be overlooked!

Build (also called the *development* or *coding* stage.) This involves writing code to fulfil the requirements gathered together during the requirements gathering and analysis stage, integration work, to ensure that all the functionality that is part of the product behaves as one cohesive unit, and solving any problems related to this.

Test. This covers the discovery of issues, faults and parts of the product that don't look, or work as intended. Testing also involves getting important feedback from users via usability testing and user acceptance testing (UAT). There are many more different types of testing for specific purposes, including *integration testing* to check that tools and software that have been connected together behave as expected, and *concurrency testing*, which verifies that software continues to work quickly and without issues arising, even when lots of people are using it.

Release. This involves getting a public version of a product, or specific functionality out to customers, or *users*. Developers will also need to make *internal releases* so that functionality can be tested and approved before it is released publicly.

Maintenance happens after the initial project to create the software has come to an end. Once a product is live and being used by customers, it needs to be maintained to ensure that it continues to operate consistently and to a high standard. Things can go wrong, or break and from time to time there will be bug fixes, or upgrades that need to be made available to users.

Now that we've reviewed the people and processes involved in developing software, in Chapter 5 we'll begin looking at how much your software will *really* cost, including hidden extras and expenses!

References

The Agile Manifesto. http://agilemanifesto.org/

Scrum Alliance. https://www.scrumalliance.org/

Agile Alliance. https://www.agilealliance.org/

CHAPTER 5

The price tag:

Establishing the true cost of software ownership

In this chapter, we'll review the direct and indirect costs of acquiring new software.

This is known as the *Total Cost of Ownership, (TCO)* which takes into account the overall cost of owning a product.

As an outcome of reading this chapter and using the costs spreadsheet provided, you will be able to create a rough estimate of your expenses. You can use this as a baseline for your budget, helping you to clarify how much your new software application will cost.

Budgeting and financial planning

A number of resources and tips for creating a shortlist of products are available in Chapter 7. However, since your budget will dictate the range of products and services available to you, we will review your software budget first.

Your costs will be allocated to one of two expense categories, *capital expenditure (capex)* or *operating expenditure (opex)*:

Capital expenditure refers to major purchases that you expect to hold for a period of a few years at least; usually high-cost, one-off acquisitions of equipment, services, goods, machinery, vehicles or computers classed as a business investment for growth, or to increase profits.

Capital expenses are reclaimed over a number of years as the item purchased begins to depreciate, or *amortize*. This could be 3-10 years or more in the case of computer software and hardware. As an example, an estimated life of 4 years would mean claiming 1/4 of the cost each year for 4 years, and therefore a shorter life-span will mean that a larger amount would be deductible against tax each year.

Operating expenditure refers to the ongoing business expenses necessary to run your business. Opex costs are tax deductible in the year they are made and are usually smaller, recurring expenses.

Software that involves buying expensive licenses up-front are likely to be classed as capex, whilst leased software paid for on a recurring basis is likely to be treated as an opex cost.

Depending on the size of your business and how it is governed, it is often easier to obtain funds for opex projects and it *may* be preferable to allocate your costs under opex where possible, in order to reclaim the full cost of the expense more rapidly.

Don't forget to consult your finance department, or accountant about your plans.

They may recommend an arrangement for the allocation of your costs against capex or opex to reduce your tax liability, and there may be matters to discuss in terms of the release of the funds that you require to purchase services, licenses or equipment.

Total Cost of Ownership

Total Cost of Ownership (also known as the Total Cost of Acquisition, TCA), considers 3 types of cost:

- **Acquisition Costs** - to obtain the product, including those to identify, select and purchase the product.
- **Ownership (or operating) Costs** - are those you will incur whilst using and running the software, such as maintenance, support and training costs.
- **Post-Ownership Costs** - include costs to dispose of, or wind-down the product at the end of its life. Note that compliance with regulations may mean paying for data to be wiped from databases or even for hardware to be completely disintegrated to protect

customers' data.

Your software costs will also include product liability costs, including costs linked to reduced productivity due to system failures, malfunctions, miscalculations, and customer dissatisfaction arising from an inability to serve your customers because of these issues.

This spreadsheet can be used to capture and keep track of potential costs. These can be split out into opex and capex specific costs if needed.

Expense item	Capex or Opex?	Year 1	Year 2	Year 3	Year 4	Year 5	Total
License fees	TBC						
Monthly subscription costs	TBC						
Maintenance	TBC						
Support costs	TBC						
Configuration costs	TBC						

You can access the full version of this *Total Cost of Ownership spreadsheet*, which includes many more expense items, here: http://bit.ly/resource2-TCO.

You are likely to be charged for the work a service provider does for you that requires additional effort from their employees.

Be sure to ask about the *maximum number of billable hours* the company could charge for on a weekly basis, and ask for standard costs per hour, or per day for tasks such as customisation, configuration, consultancy, business analysis, project management, testing, training and other services listed in your costs spread sheet.

Sometimes charges are expressed in *man hours* or *man days,* so check how many hours or days of these services customers buy on average and how many "men" are usually assigned to each task. You will then be able to multiply this by the estimated number of hours, or days to get an idea of costs.

For example, if 2 people are assigned to you from Monday to Thursday and 3 on Friday, that is 11 man days:

2 people x 4 days = 8.

3 people x 1 day = 3.

8+3 =11.

Given that in <u>*5 days*</u>*, you have had* <u>*11 days'*</u> *worth of work done, you can see that you may need to keep a close eye on how many people are working for you, and at what rate!*

As you might expect, the cost of a "man" will vary according to their skills; a more junior programmer will typically cost less than a senior counterpart. Because billing rates for staff are variable, some companies use a calculation method based on *blended days*, which assumes an average cost across a range of personnel whose time is billed to clients at different rates.

Estimating the cost of expansion

Anticipating future business growth is important. Let's look at some of the implications.

By how much do you expect your headcount to grow in the next 6, 12 or 24 months?

Increasing staff numbers can affect your requirements for *data storage, bandwidth and hardware equipment*, (points that we discussed in chapter 3) but how much will *extra software licenses* cost you?

Here are some questions to think about:

- If you are buying your software, would it be better to be charged *per head* for licenses and have *named user* or *workstation agreements*, or a *site license* that covers your whole company, or a particular site?
- Would *concurrent licensing* be more economical based on your software usage patterns?
- What about subscription based software? How will your running costs escalate if you increase your consumption of the services provided? What if you have more staff, need more storage, or make more transactions?
- What are the costs of these different license options anyway? When would it be cheaper to choose one versus another?
- If the price difference between one service package and the next is significant, will you be able to afford to continue with the product at the higher price bracket? How long do you think it will take you to graduate to a more expensive plan?

Avoid tying yourself into an expensive financial arrangement. Run the numbers on some hypothetical scenarios based on your projections for growth, and if some options start to look expensive or unsustainable, it may be best not to proceed with them.

Armed with this information and an understanding of the options that exist, you should be far more confident in negotiating licensing terms which suit you!

TCO - SaaS vs. On-Premises (Self-hosted) solutions

When is it more cost effective to opt for one type of software and hosting arrangement vs. another?

Research has been conducted on this topic, but much of the data available is focused on SaaS vs. on-premises costs and does not include more granular research into the differences between SaaS, bespoke software, on-premises solutions, colo services and other cloud based managed services - all valid choices discussed in chapters 3 and 4.

There are many variations and variables that we might consider and compare. Let's look at some graphs so we can see what kind of data is available.

Fig 6 - A comparison of costs for SaaS vs. On-premises CRM software, one of the most popular types of software purchased by SMEs.
http://www.softwareadvice.com/tco/#top.

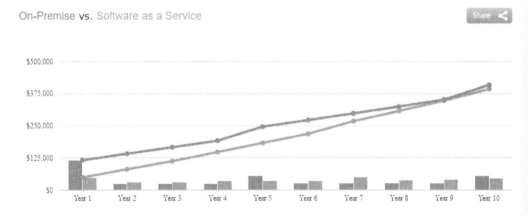

Total Cost of Ownership Calculator

This calculator lets you analyze the total cost of ownership (TCO) for an on-premise software system and a Software-as-a-Service (SaaS) system. We've pre-populated it with an example case. Adjust those fields based on pricing details you receive from software vendors.

On-Premise vs. Software as a Service

Fig 7 - SharePoint Flex: Comparing SharePoint CRM (On-premises) with Salesforce.com CRM (SaaS). http://www.sharepointcrmtemplate.com/blog/wp-content/uploads/2014/11/SPCRM-and-Salesforce-TCO-resized-600.png. http://sharepointflex.com.

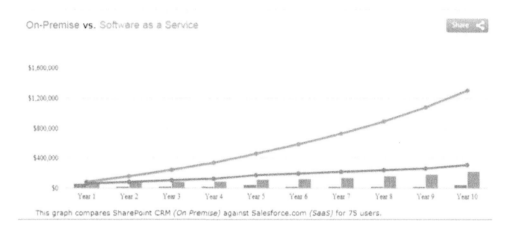

Figs 8 and 9 show ERP software and deployment costs for a very small business and a medium-sized business. http://erpcloudnews.com/2011/03/erp-software-cost-comparison-on-premise-saas-and-hosted/

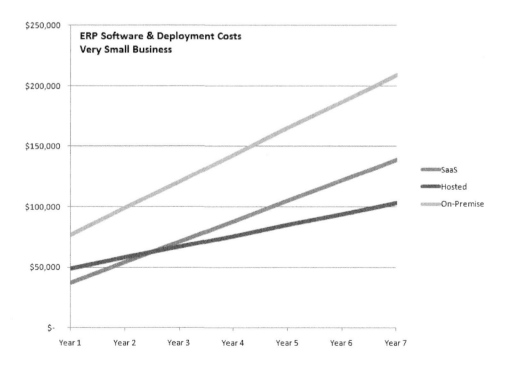

Fig 9 - ERP costs for a medium-sized business.

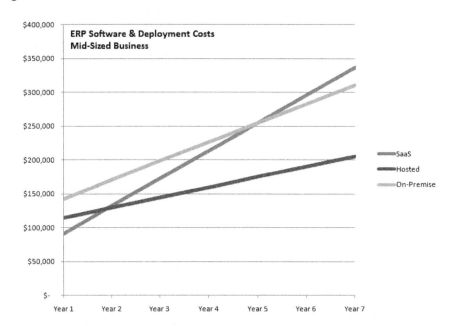

In figure 6, after 10 years, the SaaS option is slightly cheaper than the on-premises option, whilst in fig 7, SaaS costs start to race ahead of the on-premises option after year 3.

In figure 8 the managed hosted service becomes cheaper than both SaaS and on-premises options for very small businesses after approximately 2.5 years, with the on-premises option the most expensive of the three by some margin. In fig 9 the hosted option is cheaper once the company reaches year 2 of "ownership," with the SaaS option becoming more expensive than the on-premises option in year 5.

Sometimes comparisons do not provide, (or explain) all the underlying assumptions that were considered. There are numerous questions that we might ask about the information provided:

- How much did all the *equipment* cost?
- What about *salaries and personnel costs* for configuration or customisation services?
- What price was paid for *licenses*, or in *recurring fees* for hosting, or for the SaaS solutions?

- How much did *training* cost?
- What *set-up, provisioning, or installation fees* (Chapter 3), were paid upfront?
- Are the costs that were accounted based on a fixed amount each year, or do they include increases based on inflation?
- What other costs were included (or excluded)? What about post-ownership costs?

There are many unknowns here, and it is unlikely that comparisons are truly like-for like.

So, what conclusions might we draw from all this?

It is useful to take trends into account, but you should perform these calculations based on <u>your own</u> cost estimates and <u>your own</u> unique requirements. There is no magic, or universal answer.

You may, of course *choose* to accept slightly higher costs in return for the flexibility or benefits that you gain. (Another reason for having clarity on your essential and non-negotiable requirements.)

It's also worth noting again that because technology changes so quickly, it may not be advisable to tie yourself into a very long commitment, so you are free to switch to other products as your company evolves. However, for more expensive purchases, where it will typically take longer to get a return on your investment, it is common to "hold" the software for a longer period.

For larger purchases, you may wish to enlist the services of your accountant, or finance department to draw up a projection based on your requirements for years 1-3 and beyond. Give them a copy of the completed spreadsheet along with as much information as possible regarding your intentions. This will help them to calculate the TCO for each option that you want to compare.

In the next chapter, we'll look at some regulations that may apply to your business.

We'll cover a number of **existing, new and forthcoming** laws that may affect your business in 2017, 2018 and beyond, and discuss why some

software might be costly in terms of fines, or more serious sanctions –
or, on the plus side, can alleviate compliance related concerns.

References

@CloudExpo Journal. *Calculating the Total Cost of Ownership for On-Premise and SaaS Solutions.* http://cloudcomputing.sys-con.com/node/2599307

CHAPTER 6

Playing by the rules: software and its role in regulatory compliance

Legislation set by government, or other rules specified by ombudsmen, authorities, associations, or other bodies, may affect your choice of software, and how your organisation may be able to use it. You may find that you must operate with certain restrictions in place, or that there are specific procedures that your business is required to follow.

Let's review a few key terms before we proceed.

Legislation is the act of making, or enacting laws. In the UK legislation is enacted by a legislative body, such as parliament, and a single piece of legislation may be described as an act of parliament, or a statute.

Regulations are a form of legislation. If you are based in, or conduct business in Europe, it is important to be aware that regulations apply to *all* EU member states in their entirety, without the need for separate national legislation.

Regulatory compliance describes the activities undertaken by a business to comply with the laws, regulations or other rules which apply to it.

Make sure that any software you choose will add value, and certainly cause no harm in these respects. Watch out for systems that are unable (or only partially able) to comply with the relevant legislation, or other rules which apply to your business.

Which rules apply to you?

Let's start with some general resources.

For US citizens, the US Small Business Administration (SBA) provides useful links on regulations here: https://www.sba.gov/starting-business/learn-about-business-laws.

Those in the UK may need to contact a trade association, or similar bodies for advice. However, this free business support helpline may be able to direct you to the right place to find all the regulations that apply to you: https://www.gov.uk/business-support-helpline.

There is also a Gov.uk business regulations page here: https://www.gov.uk/government/policies/business-regulation. (Use the *Organisation* filter on the left-hand side of the page to help you pinpoint the right information.)

Most of the regulations we'll cover in this chapter relate to the storage, use and management of data, because businesses are responsible for how they protect and store customers' information. They will be discussed in alphabetical order:

- **Accessibility** (relevant to multiple countries under different names - usually equality or disability acts.)
- **Auto enrolment** (UK.)
- **CAN SPAM Act** (US, businesses using service providers with servers in the US.) Many countries have their own anti-spam legislation, including countries in Europe, North America and Australasia.)
- **Data Protection Act 1988** (UK.)
- **GDPR** (businesses in *any* country processing the data of EU citizens.)
- **HIPAA** (US, for businesses classed as covered entities.)
- **Making Tax Digital** (UK.)
- **PCI DSS** (global.)

Accessibility

Software should be easy to use for everyone, including those with physical disabilities, or impairments including deafness, impaired vision, blindness, colour blindness, epilepsy, dyslexia or any combination of these. Make sure that you don't unintentionally break any disability and equality laws, including the *Equality Act 2010,* because you have purchased software which cannot be used easily by all your employees, or modified to meet the needs of people with disabilities.
Ensure that staff with disabilities have access to any tools or software they need to operate the software you expect them to use in the workplace, including screen reader software like *JAWS*, alternatives to

mice for people with impaired motor skills, or other aides.

Resources:
How people with disabilities use the web by W3C, The World Wide Web Consortium, an international community which develops Web standards co-led by Web inventor Tim Berners-Lee:
https://www.w3.org/WAI/intro/people-use-web/browsing.

Auto enrolment

Many UK workers will need to be "automatically enrolled" into a workplace pension scheme by their employer.
The *staging dates* used to phase in auto enrolment and assign compliance deadlines to businesses are based on company size.
An estimated 800,000 smaller businesses with 30 employees or less, will need to complete auto enrolment for their employees by the deadline of **1st April, 2017.**

Re-enrolment; the act of putting staff back into a pension scheme will apply to larger businesses with 50 to 249 staff between **1st April 2017 and 1st April 2018.** This must be done *every 3 years* following your auto enrolment staging date. Requirements will vary, but there will be a *re-declaration of compliance* which needs to be completed and submitted to *The Pensions Regulator (TPR),* the UK regulator of work-based pension schemes.

Fig 10 - Auto enrolment staging dates.
https://www.gov.uk/government/news/new-timetable-clarifies-automatic-enrolment-starting-dates.

Employer size (by PAYE scheme size) or other description	Automatic Enrolment duty date	
	From	To
250 or more members	1 October 2012	1 February 2014
50 to 249 members	1 April 2014	1 April 2015
Test tranche for less than 30 members	1 June 2015	30 June 2015
30 to 49 members	1 August 2015	1 October 2015
Less than 30 members	1 January 2016	1 April 2017
Employers without PAYE schemes	1 April 2017	---
New employers Apr 2012 to Mar 2013	1 May 2017	---
New employers Apr 2013 to Mar 2014	1 July 2017	---
New employers Apr 2014 to Mar 2015	1 August 2017	---
New employers Apr 2015 to Dec 2015	1 October 2017	---
New employers Jan 2016 to Sep 2016	1 November 2017	---
New employers Oct 2016 to Jun 2017	1 January 2018	---
New employers Jul 2017 to Sep 2017	1 February 2018	---
New employers Oct 2017	Immediate duty	---

Resources:
You can confirm your businesses staging date using the Pension Regulator's checking service via this web page:
http://www.thepensionsregulator.gov.uk/employers/staging-date.aspx.
(Provide your PAYE reference to get an accurate date.)

The Pensions Regulator's advice for employers on automatic enrolment can be found here:

http://www.thepensionsregulator.gov.uk/en/employers.

NEST, National Employment Savings Trust is the workplace pension set up by the Government to support auto enrolment: http://www.nestpensions.org.uk/schemeweb/NestWeb/public/home/contents/homepage.html.

There are fines and penalties for non-compliance. You can find out what these are here: http://www.thepensionsregulator.gov.uk/en/employers/what-happens-if-i-dont-comply.aspx.

The CAN SPAM Act (and other Anti-SPAM legislation)

Legislation relating to spam and the sending of commercial emails may affect the way you can communicate with customers across many countries, including Australia (SPAM Act 2003) and Canada's Anti-Spam Legislation (CASL), various regulations covering the EU, plus Germany, France, India, Italy, The Netherlands, New Zealand, South Africa and Sweden and the UK (The Privacy and Electronic Communications (EC Directive) Regulations 2003, also known as PECR).

Confirm the national or international laws that you need to comply with and the measures that you may need to take, so you can check these with any software suppliers that you are considering.

Points to note:
- *The geographical location of servers is very important.* As an example, if you use an email marketing service with *servers located in the US*, then the service provider will be bound to comply with *US laws* - which means you will too. Similarly, your own country may recommend, or mandate that there are certain countries that are *not* approved to hold certain types of business data on your behalf. Because data is held on servers, you must be aware of where suppliers and service providers servers are located.
- Confirm that you are aware of the type of *individual and mass*

emails that are classed as spam in the countries that are relevant to you.

Resources for anti-spam related legislation:
Australia:
http://www.acma.gov.au/Industry/Marketers/Anti-Spam/Ensuring-you-dont-spam/key-elements-of-the-spam-act-ensuring-you-dont-spam-i-acma.
Canada: http://fightspam.gc.ca/eic/site/030.nsf/eng/home.
UK: http://www.legislation.gov.uk/uksi?title=The Privacy and Electronic Communication.
US: https://www.ftc.gov/tips-advice/business-center/guidance/can-spam-act-compliance-guide-business.

Data Protection Act, 1988, DPA

Any organisation that holds or uses information about their clients, employees or other people is legally obliged to protect that information.

The UK's Data Protection Act defines how *personal information* may be used and all businesses are required to follow data protection principles.

As a result, you will need to ensure that data is:

- Used fairly and lawfully
- Used for limited, specifically stated purposes
- Used in a way that is adequate, relevant and not excessive
- Accurate
- Kept for no longer than is absolutely necessary
- Handled according to people's data protection rights
- Kept safe and secure
- Not transferred outside the European Economic Area without adequate protection

There is stronger legal protection for more *sensitive data*, including ethnic background, political opinions, religious beliefs, physical or mental health and criminal records.

You can find the definitions of personal and sensitive data here: https://ico.org.uk/for-organisations/guide-to-data-protection/key-definitions.

In addition to preventing data being accessed from outside, it is also important to make sure data is not accessed inappropriately from *inside* your business.

If you are overhauling your software, it may be a good time to run an *audit* of IT related measures you can take to increase your compliance. For example:

- Restricting staff's access to customers' data, and keeping this to a strictly "need to know basis," so access is only given to staff who need it to do their jobs, will reduce the risk of fraud and data leaks (whereby data is moved without authorisation.) If you are buying software with *permission management (or role based)* functionality, access is sometimes controlled based on job role, level of seniority, or other permission based rules. These measures all contribute to the protection of customers' data, and therefore help to demonstrate compliance.
- Office computer systems can have printing disabled so that screens that display customers' data cannot be printed. It may also be possible to have auditing in place to log the screens that staff access and the activities they perform.
- Suspicious activities can be set up to trigger an alert with designated people within an organisation.

When you come to select your software, you may wish to ask if these sorts of services are available.

As you saw when we discussed the CAN SPAM Act, the location of the servers where your business data is held may have a significant impact on your ability to comply with certain laws. The same considerations apply to the Data Protection Act and GDPR.

As a result, it is advisable to find out where your service providers servers are located. (This includes Cloud Service Providers, SaaS companies and any organisations that hold or manage customers' data on your behalf.) Always read the terms and conditions of service carefully when you work with 3rd parties, so you know where their servers are based and therefore, which country's rules they follow.

Points to note:
To comply with the *UK data protection laws* regarding the collection, storage and safeguarding of customer data, UK companies should ideally hold their customers' data on servers located within the EEA (European Economic Area). You can find a list of countries in the EEA here: https://www.gov.uk/eu-eea

Companies based outside of the EEA may not be subject to EEA rules and therefore by allowing them to hold your data, you could be breaking the laws of your own country.

According to the Data Protection Act:
"Personal data shall not be transferred to a country or territory outside the EEA unless that country or territory ensures an adequate level of protection for the rights and freedoms of data subjects in relation to the processing of personal data."
Therefore, the European Commission has specified a number of countries based outside of the EEA deemed to offer sufficient levels of protection for personal data.

Fig 11 – Approved countries: sending personal data outside the European Economic Area (Principle 8): https://ico.org.uk/for-organisations/guide-to-data-protection/principle-8-international/.

Which countries have an adequate level of protection?

The European Commission has decided that certain countries have an adequate level of protection for personal data. Currently, the following countries are considered as having adequate protection.

Andorra	Guernsey	New Zealand
Argentina	Isle of Man	Switzerland
Canada	Israel	Uruguay
Faroe Islands	Jersey	

The European Commission's data protection website maintains an up-to-date list of approved countries.

Please note that this list is subject to change. Therefore, you may wish to review it on a periodic basis.

http://ec.europa.eu/justice/data-protection/international-transfers/adequacy/index_en.htm

---

Ask the Expert – a legal perspective

Transferring data outside of the European Economic Area, EEA

If the data is being processed outside of the EEA in a country that has not been recognised by the European Commission as having an adequate level of protection, this should not necessarily prevent you from going ahead with a software vendor, or supplier. However, you will need to factor in the cost of putting in place other measures to ensure that the transfers are lawful, for example, the model clauses for data transfers between data controllers and data processors.

Model clauses are standard contractual clauses that have been approved by the European Commission. These can either be included in the contract with the supplier or software, or entered into as a separate agreement.

You can find information on the model clauses on the European Commission's website: http://ec.europa.eu/justice/data-protection/international-transfers/transfer/index_en.htm.

Alternatives to the model clauses include the Privacy Shield, which replaced the 'Safe Harbor' programme (an agreement between the European Community and the U.S. Government to protect the data of EU citizens.)

This allows participating organisations to transfer personal data from the EU to the U.S.

Please see the Privacy Shield website for more details: https://www.privacyshield.gov/welcome.

Resources:
You can find more information about the DPA on the Gov.UK website.
https://www.gov.uk/data-protection/the-data-protection-act.

The National Archives publish all UK legislation and hold details of the DPA. http://www.legislation.gov.uk/ukpga/1998/29/contents.
Data Protection Self-Assessment. https://ico.org.uk/for-organisations/improve-your-practices/data-protection-toolkit/index.html.

General Data Protection Regulation, GDPR

The GDPR applies to *any* business that processes EU resident's data. Non-compliance carries penalties of up to 4% of a company's global turnover.

This law comes into force from *25th May 2018,* and from this date the GDPR will supersede national data protection laws, including The Data Protection Act, 1988, creating a unified set of rules across all the EU member states.

The GDPR will introduce additional data protection responsibilities for companies. The good news is that there is still some time to prepare!

Preparing your business for the GDPR

The Information Commissioner's Office, (ICO) upholds information rights in the UK.
Their website provides comprehensive information about the GDPR and is the best place to start.

The ICO states: *"For processing to be lawful under the GDPR, you need to identify a legal basis before you can process personal data. It is important that you determine your legal basis for processing personal data and document this."*
https://ico.org.uk/for-organisations/data-protection-reform/overview-of-the-gdpr/key-areas-to-consider

Continue by reviewing the following documents:

The ICO's GDPR overview.
https://ico.org.uk/for-organisations/data-protection-reform/overview-of-the-gdpr/

Preparing for the General Data Protection Regulation (GDPR): 12 steps to take now. https://ico.org.uk/media/for-organisations/documents/1624219/preparing-for-the-gdpr-12-steps.pdf

GDPR guidance in 2017.
https://iconewsblog.wordpress.com/2017/01/17/gdpr-guidance-in-2017/

Ask the Expert – a legal perspective

The Data Protection Act (DPA) and the General Data Protection Regulation (GDPR)

The DPA and the GDPR regulate the way in which personal data may be processed.

The definition of personal data is wide and covers any data that identifies or could identify a living individual: including name and contact details.

The definition of processing is equally broad and includes any use, organisation, erasure or transfer of the data.

CRM systems and several other types of software will, by their nature, process personal data. The supplier of your software may therefore be required to process personal data as part of the service they provide to you.

The DPA draws a distinction between the **data controller** – the organisation that determines the way in which the personal data will be used – and the **data processor** – that processes personal data on behalf of the data controller. The data controller is required to impose certain obligations on the data processor.

Under the DPA, it is the data controller that is subject to the compliance obligations, rather than the data processor.

If the supplier of your software is processing personal data as part of the service they are providing, you (as data controller) are required to have a written contract in place with them (as processor). Given that you will have a contract with the supplier covering the services provided, this should not of itself cause an issue, however the contract should require that the supplier (as processor) has appropriate technical and organisational measures in place to ensure data security and that they *only* process personal data in accordance with your instructions.

The DPA is not prescriptive about what technical and organisational measures will be appropriate and an informed judgement call will need to be made in each case.

It is also advisable to include some other market standard data processor obligations in the contract, including:

- A requirement for the processor to inform you of any access requests from individuals relating to their personal data and to provide reasonable assistance with them
- An indemnity from the processor to cover all your damages, losses and costs in the case where they have breached their contractual data protection obligations.

Most software supplier contracts will include a <u>financial cap</u> on their liability that relates to the value of your contract. Therefore, you should seek to exclude the data protection warranties and indemnities from the cap, given that the loss you could incur from any breach (potentially including fines from the regulator) could easily exceed the amount you are paying for the software. If you are not able to negotiate uncapped liability for a data protection breach, then you may be able to agree a separate liability cap for these types of claims.

The European Commission has produced this useful infographic on the forthcoming GDPR rules which is aimed at SMEs:

http://ec.europa.eu/justice/newsroom/data-protection/infographic/2017/index_en.htm

Compliance and security

IT security plays a big part in your ability to protect your customers' data.

Companies of all sizes are affected by cyber-attacks; therefore, it is important to keep abreast of security best-practice and to take appropriate action where necessary.

Here are some UK and US sites that offer security advice and guidance to businesses. The information provided is not necessarily country-specific, so you can make use of these resources regardless of where you are based:

- The ICO has produced a practical guide for businesses, which you can access here:
  https://ico.org.uk/media/for-organisations/documents/1575/it_security_practical_guide.pdf
- Cyberaware (Cyber streetwise) was set up by government. Their advice on protecting your business can be found here:
  https://www.cyberaware.gov.uk/protect-your-business
  https://www.gov.uk/government/uploads/system/uploads/attachment_data/file/273330/cyber_streetwise_open_for_business.pdf
- Cyber Security Guidance for Businesses. This page includes training, ways to obtain security certification for your business, and advice on guarding against fraud:
  https://www.gov.uk/government/collections/cyber-security-guidance-for-business
- Action Fraud is the UK's national reporting centre for fraud and cybercrime and operates alongside The National Fraud Intelligence Bureau (NFIB):
  http://www.actionfraud.police.uk/small-businesses-know-your-business

- The UK also has a National Cyber Security Centre.
  https://www.ncsc.gov.uk/
- The National Cyber Security Alliance (NCSA) has a website, Stay Safe Online, which offers advice to US-based businesses:
  https://staysafeonline.org/businss-safe-online/assess-your-risk/

Many of these organisations have Facebook pages and are active on Twitter.
Try using social media to keep track of the latest developments, including important notifications and warnings.

The Health Insurance Portability and Accountability Act, 1996. HIPAA (US)

The HIPAA exists to secure and protect medical records and health information.

HIPAA rules apply to any individual, organisation or agency recognised as a *covered entity.* Covered entities maintain, or transmit health information, including *PHI (Protected Health Information)* in any form.

You will find the full definition of PHI here:
https://www.hipaa.com/hipaa-protected-health-information-what-does-phi-include/.

It is recommended that any companies that help you manage or fulfil health care activities, such as a CSP (Cloud Service Provider), software supplier, or other 3rd party suppliers:

- Undergo annual independent audits of their data centre operations and cloud infrastructure and have the results of the audit checked to confirm that the CSP is truly HIPAA compliant.
- Comply with HIPAA Audit protocol, outlined here:
  https://www.hhs.gov/hipaa/for-professionals/compliance-enforcement/audit/protocol/index.html.
- Have agreed to a *business associate agreement (BAA)* if handling PHI on behalf of your business. The BAA should confirm the duties that

the supplier will perform for you and show that they agree to comply with the HIPAA requirements to protect the privacy and security of protected health information.

- PHI data should also be encrypted. https://www.hipaa.com/transmission-security-encryption-what-to-do-and-how-to-do-it/.

Make sure you understand your responsibilities (and those of companies you engage to perform any business functions for you.)

Resources:
Are you a covered entity? https://www.cms.gov/Regulations-and-Guidance/Administrative-Simplification/HIPAA-ACA/AreYouaCoveredEntity.html.

Fast facts for covered entities. https://www.hhs.gov/hipaa/for-professionals/covered-entities/fast-facts/index.html.

The HIPAA Privacy Rule and Protected Health Information (PHI). https://www.hipaa.com/hipaa-protected-health-information-what-does-phi-include/,

https://www.hhs.gov/hipaa/for-professionals/privacy/.

The HIPAA Security Rule, (SR) deals with electronic Protected Health Information (ePHI), a subset of the HIPAA Privacy Rule. https://www.hhs.gov/hipaa/for-professionals/security/.

HIPAA Survival Guide. www.hipaasurvivalguide.com/hipaa-security-rule.php.

Making Tax Digital, MTD (UK)
MTD is the UK government's initiative to transform the tax system and

bring an end to tax returns by 2020.

From July 2018, most businesses will have to begin updating HMRC on a quarterly basis and from 2019 most businesses will be expected to provide quarterly updates relating to VAT, with corporation tax to follow in the same cycle in 2020.

Consultations started in 2016, with pilots beginning in April 2017.

An important note about MTD.
The UK Government's plans to progress with Making Tax Digital were put on hold in late April 2017. For news about the Government's latest plans, keep an eye on the national news and the websites below, and check in with your accountant, or finance department for updates.
If the plans for MTD proceed in the future, then you will need to consider whether the accounting tools you use can supply information based on the new reporting cycles.

Resources:
The latest news and updates regarding MTD can be found on the government sites below.
https://www.gov.uk/government/publications/making-tax-digital/overview-of-making-tax-digital

https://www.gov.uk/government/publications/digital-reporting-and-record-keeping-for-business-income-tax/making-tax-digital-for-business

PCI DSS (Payment Card Industry Data Security Standard)

PCI DSS is a worldwide standard that helps businesses process online card payments securely and reduce debit and credit card fraud. Compliance with the standards means adhering to tight controls for the storage, transmission and processing of card holder data.

The PCI Security Standards Council, includes the major card payment companies; Visa, MasterCard and American Express. The Council have a guidance document and the importance of the standards is explained on page 4 of the document. An overview of how to comply starts on page 5:

https://www.pcisecuritystandards.org/documents/SAQ_InstrGuidelines_v3-1.pdf.

You have now reached the end of Section 1.

Section 2 is all about *execution*. The *Clarification Questions* in Chapter 8 include some questions that you can use when speaking with software suppliers about compliance and other matters discussed in this chapter, but before that, we'll start by discussing ways to locate quality software applications.

References

Legislation.gov.uk. *The official home of UK legislation:* http://www.legislation.gov.uk/help#aboutLeg

SECTION 2

EXECUTION

CHAPTER 7

Researching the market: creating an initial list of products

Welcome to section 2!

In the previous 6 chapters, we have:

- Reviewed and prioritised your **requirements** and **deal-breakers** from a **high-level strategic perspective**, down to the **day-to-day essential details, and processes** that are vital to your business.
- Considered the **relative pros and cons of different types of software**, including desktop, SaaS, enterprise software and custom-built products, and the **hosting options available**.
- Discussed the **costs** that you may face when purchasing software, and some of the **laws, or rules** that may apply to you when selecting a software application.
- You also have several documents you can use to store and manage your requirements, priorities, and project costs.

I hope you are feeling more confident and well-informed.

The objective of this chapter is to share several methods and techniques for finding quality products with the right attributes. After completing it, you should be able to identify between 5 and 10 appropriate products for your shortlist, which you can investigate further using processes that we'll discuss in Chapters 8 and 9.

Let's begin.

Creating a shortlist of software products

Here are **6** steps that you can follow to build a shortlist of products that meets your objectives.

Store your list of interesting products in the tab marked "shortlist" in this spreadsheet: http://bit.ly/resource4-comparison-shortlist.

1. Word of mouth enquiries

Ask people in your network if they can recommend any suitable products and add recommendations to your list.

Remember that staff can also be a useful source of information about the good, bad and ugly software products on the market!
If you have an IT department, some staff may even have been involved in projects to implement, or integrate products that are of interest to you. Their anecdotes, and knowledge about the outcome(s) experienced by previous employers could provide invaluable insights you might not otherwise have had.

2. Web-based research

Do some "desk research" using Google or Bing to find software and service providers.

To find more products that might be suitable and to get a sense of the "buzz" around different products, try a description of the tool plus the words, *top, popular, best, best of breed,* or *leader* e.g. *top CRM, popular CRM, best CRM, best of breed CRM, CRM leader* and possibly your country; *CRM leader UK / USA* etc. to find products that are well-established, or market leaders in your geographical region.

Other searches that will bring up a good mix of options include looking for specific products by name, or by searching for the brand name, or type of product you are interested in, alongside the word software, e.g. *Salesforce CRM, CRM software.*

Sometimes the search terms that bring back good results can be a bit on the "techie" side, so you may wish to run searches including the words *web app, web application, SaaS* or *apps* e.g. *Business Intelligence web apps, Business Intelligence web applications, Business Intelligence SaaS,* or *Business Intelligence apps* (which will bring back software applications for the web, and not just mobile apps).

Identifying consultancies, service providers and partners.

When searching for 3rd party suppliers that might sell, or implement a particular product, it may be helpful to search for the type of product you want by brand name, plus the word *consultancy,* or *partner* to find companies that may be trained or recommended by software vendors to implement the product. E.g. *Microsoft Power BI partner.*

Partners usually sell, or install products on behalf of a software vendor.

The App Exchange website holds a list of partners and consultants. Many of them have been reviewed - you can find a list here: https://appexchange.salesforce.com/consulting/top.

Some partners are certified by the software vendors they work with, so look out for badges and banners announcing this information on partners' websites.

If you are looking for companies to *host* software for you, then use the search terms *CSP* or *Cloud Service Provider, managed service provider, colocation services, colo services, managed hosting,* or *data centre,* plus your country, or alternatively include the name of any major cities close to your business that you can travel to, if necessary. If you are looking for a colo service, you may need to visit the data centre from time to time, so avoid inconvenient locations if possible.

3. Use existing research on products and software vendors.

Utilise Gartner's Magic Quadrants

Gartner, the world leader in information technology research produces the Gartner Magic Quadrants, that can be used to assess the players in a particular technology space. The Magic Quadrants consider the capabilities and strengths of the players in specific tech markets, leading to their classification as *challengers, leaders, niche players or visionaries* and are updated on a regular basis.

According to Gartner, their Magic Quadrants are: "a culmination of research in a specific market, giving you a wide-angle view of the relative positions of the market's competitors."

Gartner also offer vendor ratings and a range of other paid services. You may be able to obtain samples of these ratings by Googling *Gartner Magic Quadrant*, the *name of the market,* plus *the current or previous year* for the latest version of the quadrant, e.g. *Gartner Magic Quadrant CRM 2016.*

You can see a 2016 Magic Quadrant for CRM Customer Engagement Centre here:
https://www.gartner.com/doc/reprints?id=1-32AEZIA&ct=160331&st=sb.

Fifteen weighted categories are used to assess the companies that are placed on each quadrant. You can find more information about the methodology and criteria used here:
https://www.gartner.com/doc/3188318/markets-vendors-evaluated-gartner-magic,
http://www.gartner.com/technology/research/methodologies/research_mq.jsp.

There is also a list of Magic Quadrants for different business tools, along with the date they were last updated, here:
http://www.gartner.com/technology/research/methodologies/magicQuadrants.jsp.

Best-of-breed / best-in-class software
Gartner's Magic Quadrant approach recognises the different strengths that vendors have and is a departure from trying to "crown" products as overall *best of breed / best-in-class,* which means that they are considered to be the best software product in a particular category.

Businesses often purchase software from different vendors in order to obtain the best-of-breed offering for each type of software required. For instance, a customer might purchase human-resource (HR) software from one vendor, and finance and accounting software from another, instead of buying an *ERP, enterprise resource planning software product* which includes both types of software as available modules.

Why? Well, despite ERP vendors offering many applications in a single package, or via a choice of *software modules,* not every application available in the suite will be best-of-breed.

Try to strike the right balance between convenience and quality, and make sure that each module that you intend to use covers ALL the essential functionality to meet your needs. Look for alternatives if this is not the case.

Searches on software comparison sites

Software comparison sites are a very useful resource when selecting new tools. The aggregated product reviews and summaries of the functionality available make research convenient and time-efficient.

Take your list of promising products found via steps 1-3 and search for the products, plus the word *review* using Google or Bing to see what you can find out. Alternatively, search for each product using the comparison sites' search functionality, or by looking through the lists of software categories available on each site.

Some of the big software comparison sites include:

- **Capterra,** which offers business software reviews and infographics to help you find the right tool(s) for your business: http://www.capterra.com.
- **G2crowd,** which allows comparisons to be drawn between different software and service providers by displaying user ratings and other data collated by the company: https://www.g2crowd.com.
- If the product is right, but the price is wrong, or you find some promising software and wish to find other applications just like it, try **AlternativeTo**: http://alternativeto.net/software/geniuslink/. You can also try Googling *alternatives to company x, or software y* and

competitors of company x or software y.

- **TrustRadius** publishes the reviews and ratings posted by its professional community: https://www.trustradius.com.
- **AppExchange** were mentioned earlier, when we talked about finding consultants and partners. Owned by Salesforce, the CRM market leaders, this resource carries many reviews for products, including sales, ERP, HR, Customer Services, Finance, Marketing and Analytics: https://appexchange.salesforce.com/.
- **GetApp** can bring together several products for you to compare side-by-side. You can search and filter results and search for products that offer free versions of their software - invaluable if you require software for small, or non-business critical functions, or for smaller businesses on a tight budget. *You can also search for businesses that offer free trials, a step which I strongly recommend as part of your due diligence process.* (We'll talk more about that shortly.) https://www.getapp.com.
- **SoftwareAdvice** is powered by Gartner and offers a massive 384 categories of software that you can peruse, http://www.softwareadvice.com/uk/ (UK) or http://www.softwareadvice.com (US / International.)
- **IT Central Station**, promises access to over 10,000 reviews, but requires you to sign-in via a LinkedIn account before you can view them. As an additional service, you can create a profile on the site if you wish to do so: https://www.itcentralstation.com/.

When you identify suitable products, go directly to the **official company websites** to confirm features and pricing.

Pitfall

Minimise risks to your business: embrace *leading edge* software and avoid *bleeding edge* software.

To avoid issues, hang back from using brand new, or more experimental products as replacements for your core, or major systems.

This is not to say that there is anything wrong with them – there can be great advantages to being an "early adopter" - it may give you a competitive edge, or you may receive a discount or other benefits, but on the downside, issues and bugs in new versions of a vendor's software could disrupt your business activities and processes.

Being among the first to try a product also means being the first to experience its problems. Therefore, playing it safe and waiting until others have "found" any remaining bugs and issues can be a good strategy.

The same applies to software updates that you have a choice of accepting immediately, or putting on hold for a short time. Please note that some security updates, bug fixes and remedies may be urgent, but otherwise you may wish to adopt the same tactic before accepting any changes to your software.

Software vendors usually outline the contents of software updates in their *release notes*. Release notes include details of bug fixes, updates and new functionality, so if in doubt, check these notes and speak to your software vendor before coming to a decision. If you do decide to use a new software product, ensure you have a backup plan in place to minimise disruption should things go wrong and test the processes you expect to use *thoroughly* before you leap!

You can find more tips for managing project risks in Chapter 10.

4. Vendors' websites

Vendors' websites can be a really mixed bag. Some are very transparent about their services, product features and pricing and well...some aren't!

In some sectors, there is a lot of snooping which goes on amongst competing companies, which leads to them being cagey about their products and pricing. Unfortunately, this makes gathering information more complicated than it should be.

Whilst visiting websites, look out for the following:

- Product demonstration videos
- PDFs, documents, annotated screenshots and guides
- Product feature pages
- Frequently asked questions (FAQs)
- Help or support pages (the more organised and customer-friendly these are, the better)
- Customer discussion forums
- Product related blogs which address customers' challenges and offer advice and tips
- "How to" training videos, or webinars that customers (and prospective customers) can sign up for, or view on a website
- Pricing pages
- Technical specification details
- Evidence of the software being available as a mobile app, or being usable on mobile devices, if this is important to you

These will give you a better idea about the product and its features, the range of services offered by the vendor, the product's user interface and the amount of help and support available.

FAQs and support pages can be very revealing. They will show you where customers face challenges when using the product. They are also an easy way to find out what the software is *not* able to do: FAQs usually contain at least a few questions to which the answer is that the product does not, or cannot perform certain tasks. This information may help you rule out certain products if the range of functionality offered is unacceptable to your business or team.

You may wish to call, email or fill in a contact form to get more information, or to book an appointment for a demonstration. Drafting a standard, reusable enquiry email that requests further information and a product demonstration may help you save time.

If you book any private demos, then you may wish to arrange for members from your committee (if you formed one back in Chapter 2) to join you. (Usually these will be held via an online webinar, unless the company has agreed to visit your place of business.)

When reviewing pricing pages, you may wish to update the *Total Cost of Ownership spreadsheet* from Chapter 5. If you note down the various prices displayed by different vendors, you will find it easier to compare the cost of one product vs. another.

Project pitfall

Identify technical deal breakers as quickly as possible.

Companies often publish *technical specifications* for their products.

These are prerequisites which inform you about hardware or software requirements that you should have in place before implementing their software, such as a specific type, or version of an operating system, or recommended use of a particular web browser, or database.

This information is provided for good reason, and I have personally seen cases where very subtle changes between a vendor's recommendations and a customer's technical set-up resulted in their software application repeatedly crashing.

Keep an eye out for information about tech specs on vendors' websites and ask all the companies on your shortlist to confirm what their tech specs are.

You should know as soon as possible if purchasing a product will result in you having to make internal changes, or needing to purchase additional software or hardware to support it. This is likely to increase your TCO, so be clear about the work involved before you commit to the product.

---

5. Online videos

Video-based product reviews and product demonstrations can be a great way to conduct research and gather more "warts and all" information about a tool.

Sometimes videos are uploaded by the company that owns the product, but others also post "how-to" videos online which answer common questions about products or services.

To find videos, search via Google or Bing using the key words *"How to use"* or *"How to [insert activity or business process that is of interest to you]"* and the product, or brand name of interest. For instance, *"How to save contacts in Salesforce CRM,"* then click on the *Videos* tab.

Fig 12 – Searching for video-based information.

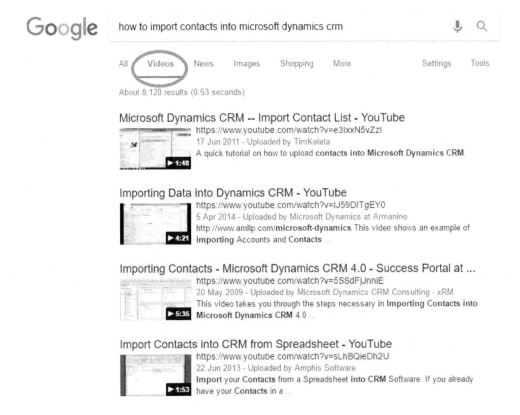

You are likely to find a mix of videos from websites, as well as from top video hosting sites such as *YouTube, Wistia* and *Vimeo.*

The great thing about these sites is that after you watch the first video, you may receive recommendations about other "how to videos" on the same topic, which should introduce you to new, but relevant products and give you a detailed view of what they look like *and* how they work!

Take note of attributes of the software such as:

- **Load times and application performance** - each time the presenter clicks buttons in the application, how long does it take before the application responds? Does it seem slow?
- **User interface** - consider the intuitiveness and layout of the product. Do you like what you see? Can you easily follow the steps the presenter is taking, or would you consider it impossible to use the product without someone to talk you through what to do and where to click? As someone who works alongside developers to create and deliver software, I don't have much patience with poorly designed products. Building products that are poorly labelled and difficult to use and understand is not at all customer-centric.
  A product that requires lots of training or is not easy to use should be cut from your list, if getting a quick return on your investment is a priority.
  If you can anticipate the buttons to be clicked next, or the process seems logical, that is a positive sign.
- **Deal-breakers** - during these product demos, the presenter will often talk about what the app *can't* do and its disadvantages and limitations. This can be useful to confirm if certain software must be cut from your list because there are deal-breakers and the product cannot deliver one or more of your "must haves."

Now, pause and reflect!

Now you've researched and qualified several products, take your requirements and notes from the previous chapters and confirm that the products you've been considering up to this point all fit your criteria and fulfil your "must have" business requirements.

Next, shortlist between 5 and 10 products to progress with. If you have less than 5 products, repeat steps 2-5 again to find more. (It's best if your shortlist isn't too short – it's common for some products to fall off your list as you discover more subtle snags.)

Store your list of interesting products in the tab marked "shortlist" in this spreadsheet: http://bit.ly/resource4-comparison-shortlist.

Pro Tip
The Parking Lot.

What should you do if you need to manage conflict, or strong characters during the software selection process? Try using the *Parking Lot* technique to "park" ideas and debates, to help you stay on track during meetings and discussions.

Use the parking lot for:

- Points that are useful, or important, but are off topic, and may require their own separate meeting.
- Points that members of the group feel strongly about (*whether relevant, or not*), which may derail your meeting (or even your entire project) unless they are managed.
- Topics where there is significant division, or disagreement.

Use a flipchart, spreadsheet or whiteboard to capture the details.

The parking lot is inclusive - it allows everyone to feel heard. Points are captured in writing and can be included in meeting minutes.
This approach also avoids disruption in meetings, and agenda hijacking (what a great phrase!) when there are other pressing matters to discuss.
Arrange follow-up meetings to address parking lot items and to review the points that have been raised.

If there are people who have very strong feelings about certain points, you can put the onus on them to do research, or collect data to support their points. Allocate a time slot in a future meeting where they may present their case to the committee and consider how you will decide whether to take the point forward, or not.

Will the decision be made by the committee, by you, or by other individuals?

The Parking Lot:

1. Comment from:	Notes:	Action / follow-up:
2. Comment from:	Notes:	Action / follow-up:
3. Comment from:	Notes:	Action / follow-up:
4. Comment from:	Notes:	Action / follow-up:
5. Comment from:	Notes:	Action / follow-up:

You can find a copy of the Parking Lot template here:
http://bit.ly/resource3-parkinglot

6. Free trials

Free trials are an excellent way to reduce your investment risk and increase your chances of selecting a great product for your business. *Getting hands-on with a product takes you beyond theory and surface-level details, to the practicalities of what it will be like to use the product on a regular basis.*

Trials are often described in different ways by different vendors; SaaS companies tend to offer 7, 14 or 28 (or 30) day free trials, others offer no free access, but have 30-day money back guarantees, whilst some offer *trial license*s for the product, or *sandbox* environments that can be downloaded and accessed with a code or *product key,* or via a website.

Plan your approach before starting the trial so you can take full advantage of it during the time available - especially where trials only last a few days.

Refer to the business requirements assessment you completed in Chapter 2 and work your way around the product, looking at the menu options available as you pass through different screens and attempt the core activities. Start with those that you value *most highly first,* then ask yourself:

- How do the processes in the trial system compare with the way(s) you do things currently? Are these differences positive or negative?
- Are processes logical?
- Does the product respond reasonably quickly to clicks and commands?
- Do you think staff will be able to learn how to use it easily? Do you think staff will like using it?
- Does the product cover all your "must haves" to a high enough standard?
- What issues or drawbacks did you find? Is there anything that can be done to minimise their impact?
- If relevant, download and check the mobile app version of the product. You should also check to see how the product looks and operates as a web page accessed via a smartphone. *Functionality and ease of use can vary dramatically on mobile devices – don't assume the experience will be identical to that seen on a laptop or office computer!*
- How does the product handle compliance related requirements? Is this good enough to meet your needs?
- Are the benefits significant enough to proceed with the product? Why / why not?
- What's missing? Did you identify any deal breakers? If they really are deal-breakers, then cut the item from your list, despite its other positive attributes.

Have the right people available to use and test the product. Aim to involve members of staff who know and understand the processes and tasks to be performed, and have the experience to spot potential issues. Ask them to answer each of the bullet points above as a short "report" on their impressions of the software, including any other comments that they would like to make.

If you have any queries after your trial, contact the software vendor for clarification.

Comparing suppliers based on documentation

If you are buying a high-priced system and you'd like to put a more formal procedure in place, consider using the following documents to compare suppliers:

An RFI (Request for Information) is normally used to collect information in writing about a supplier and their services and capabilities. The information gathered can be compared and used to form a shortlist. You might then ask for the remaining contenders to submit an *RFP, a Request for Proposal.*

Alternatively, you may choose to request an *RFP* in the first instance, but in that case, you would miss the opportunity to gather additional information before making a decision.

An RFP asks suppliers to submit a proposal in a specified format that contains enough information for you to select a "winning" product or service from those submitted. The RFP may include the following sections:

- A confidentiality, or non-disclosure agreement.

- Your company information.
- An explanation of the project you want to undertake and the services you require.
- The process you intend to follow, the time-frame allocated for the selection process, and when you hope to start the work.
- Your requirements. (Include your "must haves", deal-breakers and other information gathered during the business requirements assessment process you worked through in Chapter 2 to help suppliers to understand your needs.)
- Your budget (you may ask the supplier to provide a breakdown of what they would charge based on the requirements that you have supplied.)
- How and when suppliers should submit their proposals, and your submission deadline.

RFTs (Request for tender) and ITTs (Invitation to tender) are of a similar ilk to the RFP and invite companies to bid to supply you with their services.

A *statement of work (SOW)* - is a vital document for clarifying and confirming your project deliverables, so all parties are clear on what is going to happen, when it will happen, the duration of the work, how the tasks will be completed and who will be responsible for completing them. In some cases, SOWs are legally binding documents.

A SOW may accompany a request for proposal (RFP), and will specify:

- The background to the project
- The project's objectives
- The scope of the work
- The requirements, with tasks and deliverables described, along with their relative priorities
- The location where the work will take place
- Timings - the high-level phases, or stages of the project and any key project milestones
- The resources, roles and responsibilities of the parties involved
- Any standards or regulations that must be adhered to

- Special requirements, such as hardware and software that might be needed
- Terms and conditions
- Confidentiality and non-disclosure documents
- System requirements
- Technical requirements
- The approach
  - The approach to quality assurance, outlining how the product will be tested, by whom and how you will check the product so that you can confirm that the work has been delivered as expected
  - Assumptions
  - Inclusions and exclusions, such as upgrades, updates, maintenance and support
  - A payment schedule
  - The process for managing any changes and requests that affect the scope of the project

Make sure you know what will happen and when, and how each element of the SOW will work.

Ask the Expert – a legal perspective.

Contract structure

A statement of work, or SOW, may be presented by the software vendor along with a request for proposal (RFP) before contracts are signed.

Depending on the project, the software vendor may seek to put in place a *framework, or umbrella contract* which refers generally to the provision of services and covers key legal points, such as:
- Ownership of intellectual property rights, IPR
- Warranties and indemnities (contractual promises)
- Risk allocation (the limits and exclusions of each party's liability under the contract)

- Remedies (the contractual solutions available to each party in the event of a breach of contract)
- Governing law (the local laws which are to be followed when enforcing the agreement)

Under this structure, the terms of the framework contract will apply to the statement of work (and any other SOWs that are entered into by the parties – for example, you may have separate SOW contracts in place to cover different phases of your project, or key deliverables.)

If this is the case, SOWs will cover project-specific matters only, as the headline legal terms will have been included in the framework contract.

The first point to check then, is whether the SOW that is provided will be governed by a separate framework agreement, or if there will be just one contract.

You may decide to invite software houses, consultancies or suppliers to speak, or meet with you, to discuss their software or services in more detail. Therefore, in the next chapter, we'll look at a number of *Clarification Questions* that you can use during your conversations with these 3rd parties.

The knowledge you gain from their answers should help you to reduce your shortlist to between 2 and 5 possibilities before completing your due diligence checks in Chapter 9 and making a final decision!

CHAPTER 8

The beauty parade:
5 steps to a quality software shortlist

"I suppose it is tempting, if the only tool you have is a hammer, to treat everything as if it were a nail."
- Abraham Maslow

We've reached the stage of the selection process referred to as "the beauty parade," a light-hearted reference to what is usually a "parade" of demonstrations and pitches delivered by companies to win your business, usually followed by a Q&A and an opportunity to clarify outstanding queries.

It's a great analogy. However, your job is to look beyond the exterior. Many products will look acceptable at face value, so it is necessary to explore the substance behind initial appearances.

We will get to the substance through asking probing questions and putting assumptions to one side.

To avoid committing to buy the wrong product, try not to be wowed, or distracted - stay focused on confirming that you can put either a tick √, or cross X, and a comment against each of your "must have" requirements as a first priority.

Consultancies may not be keen to point out the deficiencies in their software and services, so be prepared to pursue clarification on the matters that are important to you.

Don't fill in any blanks based on what you *think* is correct, make sure *all* decisions are based on facts.

Taking control of the process

Despite your best intentions, it is easy to find yourself in a situation where you have spent hours being pitched to, but don't yet have the information you need from the vendor, who has driven the meeting according to their own agenda.

To avoid this, there are some things you can do to make sure that the process is effective for all concerned:

Have a selection process.

Suppliers will want to know how many hoops they will have to jump through before they can seal the deal, so you'll be asked about your selection process.

You may wish to use this **5**-step process as a guideline for assessing each product / supplier:

1. **Verbal checks** - get a verbal description and confirmation of what the product can do and how this is achieved. Try and get a definitive answer – either "yes, it does", or "no, it doesn't"! (Of course, you may also be told about other "similar" functionality too.)
2. **Visual checks** - make sure you *see* the software "in action" and watch it perform each process and activity you consider to be a "must have."
3. **Manual checks** - take advantage of free trials or demonstration versions of the product to get a feel for how easy processes and activities are to complete.
4. **Written confirmation** - ask for important details to be confirmed in writing, along with the answers to any questions that you raise. Focus on your "must haves" and deal breakers as the priority, and compare the documents you have received from service providers, such as quotes, tender or proposal documents.
5. **Due diligence checks** - these checks involve researching the product and the supplier. We began the *due diligence* process in Chapter 7 and will continue with it here, and in Chapter 9.

You may have already completed some of these checks. If not, you should be able to cover more of them during the beauty parade, followed by **written confirmation** from the software vendors, and further **due diligence** from you, or other members of your company as the next step.

Agree on an agenda and brief companies before you have any meetings.

Most companies will appreciate it if you can give them some idea of the functionality, features and services that are of particular interest to you.

Unless there is a reason why you cannot share this information, then you should provide these details to all the companies involved in advance of your meetings. You may wish to ask for a non-disclosure agreement to be signed to keep information about your company and its plans confidential. See Chapter 9 for more information.

Some presenters will be slower than others at connecting the dots between your requirements and their product on the fly, so advance notice should hopefully mean better preparation - and a better presentation.

Give the presenter a time-slot.

Depending on the length of your meeting, allocate between 30 to 45 minutes for a demonstration and sales pitch.

The vendor / service provider should have the opportunity to showcase their product or services, but if you want to avoid wasting time, or overlooking important information, try to get all the facts needed to decide whether a product should make it onto your final shortlist during the presentation.

After the pitch, inform companies that the rest of the meeting will be used exclusively for showing you the items that you have asked to see and a Q&A session to address your queries.

Remain focused on the items that will assist you in fulfilling the "must haves" required for your business, or team and not the non-essentials that look good, but are a distraction. If you aren't able to gather all the information you need, you may require a follow-up session to cover the gaps in your knowledge. Don't be tempted to take a product, or service forward as a potential "winner" if you're not sure that it meets your fundamental needs.

Make sure you are not sold the wrong tool to solve the business challenges that you face, and don't let anyone convince you that you require a product, just because that's all they have to sell!

5 things about the beauty parade to be aware of:

1. **What you see isn't always what you get.** If you are being shown an enterprise product, it will have been customised or configured and set up specifically for customer demonstrations to present the product in the best light. It's like a show home on a development of newly built properties, with everything looking its best. The basic product you buy may not closely resemble the "demonstration version" that you see at the beauty parade!

2. **Some products take a *lot* of work before they are usable.** Unfortunately, you won't be able to see how much effort it took to get the product set up and ready for the demonstration. Some features will come "out-of-the-box" (i.e. these items look and operate as demonstrated, without any further work or adjustments), but others will require development work, (customisation) or less complex manual adjustments (configuration). It's important to know the difference, because customisation equates to time and money and configuration too, to a lesser extent!

3. **The people you get to know at the start of the process may not be around *after* you buy the product.** Depending on the size of the company you are working with, they may employ pre and post sales consultants. Generally, *pre-sales consultants,* who are skilled in setting up the product and presenting it, will manage customer demonstrations and sales pitches. If they are successful, they will hand over to a *post-sales team*, who will get much deeper into the work of clarifying your requirements, making sure any extra work you request is delivered, and guiding you through the stages of the purchase process, including contracts, project and payment milestones.

4. **You'll be deciding on a product and a vendor as a package.** *Make sure you're happy with both.* It can be a real shame when one seems great, whilst the other is not quite right. If you like the company and they can supply other products, ask them to recommend and then demonstrate some alternatives that might meet your needs. (Even if this happens, stick to the same process for assessing all the products that you are considering.) If you like the product and not the supplier, revisit Chapter 6 and look for alternatives to it, or see if the software can be obtained through another software partner.

5. **Objectivity is important.** To keep the selection process neutral, it's best to provide a rating for each product and vendor based on what you see and hear. This will allow you to review the contenders purely based on their scores.

Now let's look at the Clarification Questions.

The "Clarification Questions"

Use these questions to clarify important points and to bring hidden costs, inconveniences and challenges to the surface. Ask them during your beauty parade meetings, or alternatively, send them out as questions, wait for the responses and then proceed further with those who provide acceptable answers!

Consider keeping score: score your "must haves" as a priority, and use your spreadsheet to log how close each software application is to the ideal for each of your main criteria. Ask yourself whether the functionality available meets your expectations, and rate the ability of the product to meet your needs to a high, medium, or low standard, or not at all.

You can download a copy of all the questions here:
http://bit.ly/resource5-clarification.

A product comparison spreadsheet has been provided for you, here:
http://bit.ly/resource4-comparison-shortlist. There is plenty of space for your notes and observations and you can give products a score out of 10.

*For each feature, or service you wish to query, complete your **verbal and visual checks** where possible. Ask for confirmation, and to actually **see** how the software will fulfil your requirements. For instance:*

"We want to be able to [insert goal.] Please demonstrate, and talk us through how your system supports this / will help us achieve this…"

Repeat this question until you can tick off all your must have requirements, and have addressed your most pressing concerns.

ROI warning!

Configuration, or customisation?

Would you find it comforting to know that each product that you are considering fulfils most, or all of your essential requirements *without* significant additional cost?

If so, the question: **"Does that require *configuration*, or *customisation*?"** is a powerful one to use during conversations with software vendors. When software features are discussed, confirm which functionality:

1. Comes "out-of-the-box" and will work immediately after installation.

2. Will need minor manual adjustments that your own staff can make without assistance.

3. Requires input from the provider, or vendor to set up, such as code changes, (customisation) or manual configuration (config) by a specialist, which will usually incur a fee.

Once you consider the amount of config and customisation required overall, you will get a sense of the amount of work involved in adapting the software to make it fit for use and whether you're likely to face lots of added expenses.

If you know the approximate time it would take to do the work and the company's fees per day or per hour, then you will be able to calculate a rough cost. You can compare these costs against the other products that you are considering.

As much as you may like the software, if there are "musts" that will require significant effort and expense before they can be delivered, it may

---

> be wise to keep looking.
>
> **Quality out-of-the-box functionality is usually a bigger benefit than functionality that requires config or customisation, unless this extra work is very minimal.**
>
> *If a product is missing a feature that you need, ask if there are any workarounds available - if there is an acceptable way to overcome a limitation in the software, then you may not have to rule the product out completely.*

*   *   *

The Clarification Questions

Data migration, management and storage

- How will we get our [insert type, or name of data] data into the new system? Please explain the steps involved and the options available.

- Is there a fee for doing this? If so, what is it?

- Is there any specific equipment that we will need to buy in order to migrate our data?

- Is it possible for us to download / export our data back out of the system if we want to? Please explain the process.

- How and where will the data be stored? In which countries are your servers located?

- Can you help us to clean our data [and get rid of (or archive) duplicates and "dead" data] before we transfer it into the new system? *(This could be an opportune time to do this type of task.)*

Some data transfer processes can be quite complex, (or to be more frank, a pain in the neck) so make sure you understand exactly what's involved in getting data into (and out of) the system.

The characteristics of the data centres run, or used by CSPs and software vendors may differ, so ask each provider about the protocols they have in place.

The location of the servers holding your data could have an impact on your ability to comply with GDPR and other regulations. You may also have to comply with regulations that apply to the country where servers are located, as well as the laws of your own country. (Please note the approved countries listed in Chapter 6.)

Disaster recovery (DR), backup and recovery of data

- What DR (Disaster Recovery) mechanisms do you have in place?

For risk management purposes, you should be aware of how your data is going to be stored and backed up and how it will be safely retrieved in the event of any software, networking or hardware failure caused by man, beast or Acts of God!

System reliability / availability

- What level of *system uptime* do you guarantee?

- What is your routine for taking the system down for maintenance work? How much advance warning will we receive and at what hours of the day, or night will this happen?

Because no system is perfect, service providers cannot guarantee your system will always be up and running. As a result, your software will be subject to a degree of unplanned outage time or downtime. No-one knows when this will occur – it's unplanned!

Each supplier's service level agreements (SLA) will state the level of uptime, or availability that they can guarantee. (SLAs will be discussed in more detail in the next chapter.)

*Uptime of **99.9% to 99.99%** means that you can expect the amount of **unplanned downtime** to be between 8.8 hours and 50 minutes per year. Taking the worst-case scenario of 8.8 hours' downtime at 99.9%, and assuming you are unlucky, and that every outage happens during the* *working week, this could be 44 minutes of unexpected outages per month where you will be unable to complete business activities.*

Here are my workings:

8.8 hours = 528 minutes (8.8 x 60 minutes.)

528 minutes / 12 months = 44 minutes per month.

If this is not acceptable, consider looking for between 99.99% and 99.999% availability.

In terms of *planned outages* for maintenance and "housekeeping", a responsible B2B service provider will not take systems down from Monday to Friday during peak usage times, so I would expect systems to be maintained over the weekend or late at night as standard practice. However, this should not be assumed and if service providers have a global customer base, there may never be a good time during the week to take down a system!

Find out how each vendor manages this challenge and note any routines that might disrupt your business activities.

Please answer the question!
Take note of how your questions are handled.
It's important that vendors do their best to make sure you are well-informed and are forthcoming in explaining processes and procedures to you - including the problematic, or challenging ones!
Remind service providers that you won't proceed without responses to all the questions you've asked.
Proceed with caution if getting the "full story" proves to be difficult - consider what a business relationship would be like with a company that you need to surgically extract information from!

Integration

- Which other software, products and data does your software integrate with?

- How do [insert the names of any integrations from the previous question that are of interest] work?

- Are these integrations "out-of-the-box" or do they require configuration or customisation? Please explain the tasks involved and how long they usually take to complete.

Confirm the opportunities available and the cost and effort involved in achieving these integrations.

Pro Tip

Take note of verbal and non-verbal signals during face-to-face meetings.
As a consultant, staying attuned to people's body language is a useful skill. We all communicate non-verbally, and I've seen sales consultants indicate that there may be cause for concern without saying a word!
Watch out for revealing signals, such as puffing and exhalations (as in 'hoooomph, that won't be easy!' or, 'pfffff, I really have no idea!'), pregnant pauses and hesitation, looking flustered or worried, indirect and flowery ways of saying "no" and giving "diplomatic" answers when fielding questions about a product.
If you pick up on these, prod the issue a little more to see what you can find out!

Quality Assurance

- What are our options for trialling your product before we make a final decision?
- How will the product be tested before it is handed over to us for *UAT (User Acceptance Testing)*?
- How does the UAT process usually work?

We've talked about the value in using free trials to gain an advantage in selecting the right product.

Many companies now offer such trials, however, if you have been unable to get access to the product, ask how this can be done. You can then run the checks outlined in the free trials section (Step 6) in Chapter 7.

If you are having software configured, customised, or built for you, then it is crucial that you find out how and when your employees will be able to review the software to confirm that it has been adapted according to the agreed specifications. Always allocate sufficient time for the UAT process and use as many real-world scenarios as possible when testing – this is the best way to identify issues.

Security

- How do you protect your systems, and your customers' data from loss, theft and cyber-attacks?

- If we were to use your software, what measures would you recommend that we take as a business to minimise the risk of security breaches and hacking?

- In the event of a security breach, how and when would we be notified?

If you have a security team, you can send them the answers you receive for review so they can advise you of any flaws or concerns that they note. Depending on the type of data your company holds, this may be necessary to meet the requirements of the UK Data Protection Act, as well as the forthcoming GDPR, HIPAA and other regulations that seek to protect customers' personal data.

Take any security measures recommended by the software / hosting provider.
Additionally, ask staff to choose complex passwords which can't easily be guessed in order to protect their accounts from unauthorised use.

A mix of lower and uppercase letters, numbers and non-alphanumeric characters (if these are permitted by the software) is best.

Some software automatically forces users to update their passwords and will not allow reuse of old passwords as a security measure, but if these measures are not in place, then warn staff to change passwords regularly

(every 6 to 8 weeks at least.)

Passwords should never be shared. If an incident occurs, it will be more difficult to investigate what happened.

Reporting

If reports are important to you, the following questions will give you an overview of what may be possible:

- Can you demonstrate the product's report generating capabilities? *Note what's possible and ask about any specific reports that you need.*

- What skills are needed to create new reports / reports of type _____ [insert the type of report that interests you.] How long does this usually take? Is this config, or customisation work? *Ask to see how this is done. If there is a lot of fiddling and huffing going on, you may conclude that this is not an easy task!*

- What flexibility is there to amend these reports? Can we specify the exact dates that reports are generated? *Ask to see how this is done.*

- Can the reports be automatically generated, or is this a manual task? Can the reports be automatically emailed to specific people within our business? *If reports are hard to generate, but you only need to endure the pain once because they can be automated, would this be acceptable?*

Permissions management and auditing

- Does your tool contain permissions management functionality (to restrict the activities that different staff can perform, including creating, viewing, amending, printing, copying or deleting data)? How are these controlled, and how granular are the controls?

- Is your software able to audit staff's use of the system so we can see the date and time at which staff log in and the activities performed? Are there any alerts available?

Insurance

- Are there any types of insurance cover that you would recommend that we take out? If so, what cover / types of policy do you recommend?

- Can you recommend any insurance companies?

This will give you some idea of the types of policies and cover that may be relevant. Be prepared to do your own independent research on any companies that are recommended.

Contact the provider of your existing insurance policy to check whether it covers you against cyber-attacks, financial losses caused by power, network, or other failures, and indemnifies you against data losses or data theft.

If you are buying equipment, you may require cover for theft, damage or loss. It's advisable to check the warranty periods on the items purchased, and ask to whether they can be extended.

Hosting

- What hosting options are available?

- What services are available with each hosting option?

- Which of these services are included in the monthly or upfront cost of the software and which are chargeable extras?

- How do costs differ depending on the type of hosting that we select?

Use the blue comparison tables in Chapter 3 to identify the pros and cons of the various options. (If you have already done this, focus on finding out as much about the services that interest you as possible.)

Support and Maintenance

- What's included in your support package(s)? *Ask for a breakdown of all the packages, what they cover and their prices.*

- What flexibility is there? Which services are mandatory?

- Does your support service operate 24 hours a day, 7 days a week, 365 days a year? If not, what are the hours of service?

- What's included in your maintenance package?

- Which services are charged as extras? *(What is free, or classed as an extra may vary depending on your service package.)*

- When do costs fall due?

- How will you notify us about updates (bug fixes, code released to resolve issues) and upgrades (improvements to bring you into line with the latest version of the product)?

- Can we choose to delay an update or upgrade? *(You may recall that new software releases may still contain bugs and issues!)*

- How will any integrations and adjustments, (including customisation or configuration) that we put in place be affected by updates / upgrades?

- If we manage our own hosting what upgrade, update, support and maintenance fees would still be due? Which tasks would we have to perform ourselves?

Check exactly what you will get in terms of support and maintenance, and at what price.

It is important to clarify that any integration, customisation or configuration work you put in place will not be disrupted or jeopardised by updates and upgrades. It may seem bizarre that this can happen, but these types of issues do occur! This fact-finding process will help you discover any oddities and undesirable characteristics related to the software, service, or vendor.

There may be good reasons why services are mandatory… alternatively, you may not get a reasonable explanation as to why certain arrangements are necessary. You will need to decide whether you think this is acceptable; if you have a capable internal IT department, it might be worth asking if you can pay for support later - if you really need it.

Regulations and compliance

- Is your software / hosted service fully [HIPAA/DPA/PCI DSS - insert relevant regulation, rule or legislation] compliant?

- How will your company support compliance with the GDPR?

Select the regulations which are relevant to your business and ask about these. What level of knowledge does the supplier seem to have about the topic?

Ask them to explain their understanding of the different parts of the regulation and where relevant, how the software meets each element.

Request further information, including documentation that confirms how the service provider complies with these regulations, including the auditing of their own procedures.

Bespoke software

- What is your end-to-end process for delivering software to your clients?

- How will you estimate the work and cost involved in delivering our software?

- Can you confirm that we will exclusively own the source code for the product?

- Which project management methodology do you use? *This will help you to understand more about the philosophy of the company.*

- When will IPR, (Intellectual Property Rights) be transferred to our company?

- Is this included as a clause in your contracts? *It should be if the IPR will belong to you!*

- When will we receive the source code and how will you deliver this to us?

See Chapter 4 for more information about *bespoke software development* and Chapter 9 for further details about *intellectual property rights.*

Costs

Get unpleasant surprises out in the open as quickly as possible and avoid misunderstandings, or being drip-fed with additional expenses as you progress through the selection process!

- Could you please run through each expense we should budget for, item by item? Please explain what each expense covers and include any one-off, or set-up fees (including the cost of any initial provisioning fees, if speaking to a colo, or cloud service provider) as well as recurring costs whether monthly, annual or other.

- Are there any usage limits or exclusions for each expense item? *Do costs increase per user, or based on usage? If you are buying licenses (rather than a monthly subscription), confirm the type of license by name (site license, named user license etc.) and whether the initial license fee to be paid is a one-off cost, or whether there is an additional annual license fee.*

- Can you outline any other costs we should be prepared for as our company grows and more staff begin using the software? *Confirm whether you would be charged if you ever require more licenses and how you should go about requesting them if needed.*

- Is there any other chargeable work required to get the software up and running? Are there other products or services that might be needed before our staff can make full use of the product, or get the best results from it?

- Please talk us through any technical specifications needed to run the software. If you don't have all the items on the specifications list, you may have to pay to have these put in place.

- How much time [and money] will it take to get the product into a state where it can do _____ [insert your must haves]?

- How much do system / software upgrades cost? Is there a price difference for major, vs. minor upgrades? Please provide full details.

- Can you give us an idea of the fees and costs for years 2 and 3? Should we expect any new costs? Are any increases in price planned in the next 12 months?

Were there any missing costs not yet accounted for that will affect you now, or in the future?

*Some software can be extended by using **add-ons,** and **plug-ins** (widgets, or components that can be bolted on to existing software to enhance it) at an additional cost.*

Note down the options available and the costs involved, so you can see which products will be the most expensive overall.

Project pitfall

Be wary of yes men!

Look for service providers who don't avoid tough questions, sound like they are good problem solvers and can give examples of *how* they might use their expertise to overcome challenges – rather than those that act as if there won't be any!

Of course, flexibility and a "can do" approach is also important. Note how flexible the company seems to be. Do they try to find solutions, or is the answer always: "That's not possible," or "That will cost extra."?

Training

- What training is available and in what formats?

- What training is included / complimentary when we subscribe to use

/ buy the software, and what needs to be paid for? What is the cost?

- Where is training usually delivered? Does the cost vary depending on where training sessions are held? *If training is delivered online, can this be initiated at any time, or are there set times when sessions run? How often are these available?*

- How much time should we allocate for training?

- Is refresher / follow-up training available for those that require more help, or who missed the initial training?

- Is advanced training available so we can have some "power users" or administrators within our business?

- How quickly can sessions be booked if we want them?

- Can training be tailored to the specific needs of your company and any customisation / configuration you have paid for, or will it be generic training delivered as standard to all customers? How much would tailored training cost?

- What training will be provided to help us when software upgrades that contain new functionality are released?

- What help, or guidance is available within the software application itself? *(Inline help, where information is provided within the software application itself; usually identifiable by an ! or ? sign, can help users if they get stuck.)*

A big factor in achieving ROI is the quality of the training materials and the training delivered to your staff. If none is provided, then the onus will be on your organisation to make sure that employees can use the new software effectively.

You can find more information about reducing project risk and improving ROI through training in Chapter 10.

Human resources

- Will we get an account manager or dedicated person that we can call or email if needed? What services could they perform for us? Is there any additional cost for this service?

- If we were to proceed, who would you assign to work with us?

- What level of experience would they have?

- How do you decide who is assigned to do our customisation or configuration work for us? What happens if we feel that the people assigned to us are unsuitable?

A dedicated account manager can be a useful service.

Consider the trade-off between being assigned staff who are highly experienced and generally more expensive, and more junior staff charged out at a lower rate.

How easy does it sound to find replacement staff if you want them?

Achieving ROI and managing project risk

- In what way(s) are you able to help customers to get a quick return on their investment?

- Are you able to support customers in coordinating phased, parallel or pilot rollouts? Which approach would you recommend?

- If we required it, could you help us set up a proof of concept or prototype? *See Chapter 9 for more information about rollout and proof of concept options.*

- What are the most common issues that customers experience? *Now is the right time to ask this question!*

- What other steps could we take to reduce project risk?

Depending on the type of software and implementation method you choose, it may take slightly longer to achieve a return on your investment. Note the level of detail in the reply you receive.

If the system you are replacing is fundamental to the running of your business then beginning the project with a proof of concept, or prototype and ending the project with a software rollout that allows you to keep your "old" software running as a back-up may be very sensible contingencies.

We'll discuss these, along with other risk management strategies in more detail in Chapter 10.

Termination

- What notice period would be required to cancel our contract with you? Once a customer gives notice, what processes do you follow?

- What happens to our data if we switch to a new software supplier? Please explain the process and any costs involved.

It may be a long way in the future, but any relationship formed will not last forever!

Clarify the duration of any lock-in periods or other restrictions, consequences or inconveniences attached to ending a commercial relationship as soon as possible. Have a clear exit strategy and make sure you're familiar with your supplier's terms and conditions.

Find out if there are any direct or indirect costs involved in terminating your agreement with each service provider. Sometimes, disentangling from suppliers can be painful, questionably to make it easier to stay than to leave!

It is best to be aware of these hindrances <u>before</u> you sign any agreements.

Pitfall

Test the merchandise before committing… and avoid long-term contracts with harsh penalties for early termination.

A few years ago, I worked with an SME client who asked me to research CMS products for them.

The CMS they were using at the time was unreliable and difficult to use, but the company had signed up to a long-term support and maintenance contract that they couldn't get out of.

The only thing worse than buying a product that has a negative impact on your business is being forced to continue paying extra for it!

In this case the support package that was purchased wasn't even being used, which made bearing the cost even more frustrating.

Trialling products and putting them through some of the tests I mentione back in Chapter 7 will reduce the chances of discovering that a product is inadequate *after* contracts have been signed.

References / case studies

- Have you worked with any businesses in the same / similar industry sector to ours, or businesses that use the product in the same way(s) that we wish to use it?

- Could you please provide us with the details of two such referees that we can call, or visit?

A set of reference questions can be found in the next chapter.

It need not be a deal-breaker if a company has never worked with an organisation like yours before, but if you have requirements or business processes that will need a fair amount of customisation to be done, it may be useful to know if there are other businesses that have attempted the same thing.

Understanding the degree of success that others have had with the approach, along with the issues they faced could help you decide if a particular product (or approach) is right for you.

A company that understands your industry and the way you conduct business may be very useful.

Closing the meeting

Do you have definitive responses to every query and "must have" item on your list?

If not, ask for any outstanding items to be taken away by the vendor and followed up on a subsequent call, in a meeting, or via email.

You can send a copy of this document to companies for them to complete, along with any additional questions that you may have.

Ask suppliers to provide details of all costs associated with the purchase in writing too, including up-front costs and ongoing running and maintenance costs.

In the case of many SaaS suppliers, these details may all be on their websites, but as always, never assume. A quick email may be enough to confirm the details.

Final questions…

Based on what we've told you, please talk us through the standard process if we were to proceed with you, including:

- The customer "onboarding" process

- Contracts and agreements

- Your initial thoughts about delivery timescales

- Payment milestones

- Preparatory tasks, or activities that would need to be completed

- Based on what we're trying to achieve, what issues do you foresee? How would you recommend that we approach these challenges?

- Is there anything else we need to know, or consider about your company or your product, before we complete our shortlisting process?

What is your initial impression of the quality of the information / advice you are offered?

How willing is the company to talk about both the pros and cons of the different options available to you and the possible challenges ahead?

You can download a copy of all the questions here:
http://bit.ly/resource4-comparison-shortlist.

*   *   *

Follow-up

Often, businesses find out the downsides to working with service providers too late.

Even if you *don't* have major questions, put in a call / email to each company you're considering to see how quickly they respond and how they deal with you.

Can you get hold of a knowledgeable and helpful person on the phone, or get a decent email response within a reasonable time frame?

Do you have to hold for half an hour, pressing 1 for this, and 2 for that?

This is when you'll find out more about each company's support and customer care standards.

If you've been given direct line numbers to call during the selection process, be aware that once you become a customer you'll almost certainly be asked to call the general number like everyone else!

Pitfall

Pay attention to customer care processes

I have seen businesses paying thousands to companies on retainer and no-one ever knew if, or when they would grace the business with a response when they were asked a question!

This is totally unacceptable. Avoid entering an agreement with a company that shows signs of this kind of behaviour.

Don't proceed based on the hope that the situation will improve!

In the next chapter, we'll look at some important considerations relating to contracts, due diligence and ways to further reduce the risks involved in selecting the right software and supplier. By now you may have 1 to 3 companies to take forward for further review. However, until your due diligence is complete you may wish to hold off on communicating definite "no's" to companies that have products that you would consider using.

This is a precaution in case the information gathered during the due diligence process has an impact on your preference(s) - it's best not to burn bridges prematurely!

References

IBM knowledge Centre. *Uptime Requirements.*
https://www.ibm.com/support/knowledgecenter/ssw_ibm_i_61/rzarj/r
zarjhareqsuptime.htm

The UK Government. *Cyber Security Guidance for Business*. This page
includes training, ways to obtain certification for your business and
advice on guarding against fraud.
https://www.gov.uk/government/collections/cyber-security-guidance-
for-business
www.cyberstreetwise.com

The National Fraud Intelligence Bureau (NFIB) and Action Fraud. (Action
fraud is the UK's national reporting centre for fraud and cybercrime.)
http://www.actionfraud.police.uk/small-businesses-know-your-business

CHAPTER 9

Caveat emptor!
Due diligence, contracts and your rights

What happens when you have narrowed down your list of products and suppliers, and several have "made the cut" in terms of the features offered, costs, compliance, suitability as service providers, and their ability to provide satisfactory responses to your questions?

It's almost time to make a decision - but first, it would be beneficial to complete some due diligence checks, take up references, and review the contracts and documents that clarify the responsibilities and obligations of your supplier.

At this stage, deal-breakers and unacceptable legal clauses may become evident -unfortunately, some customers only discover these things *after* they have signed contracts.

This is a case of *caveat emptor*, or "buyer beware." It is up to you to complete your research, so you can safely clear the final hurdle.

In this chapter, we'll be discussing *Service Level Agreements (SLAs), Intellectual Property Rights (IPR), end user license agreements (EULAs), Non-disclosure agreements (NDAs)* and more!

Performing due diligence checks

Due diligence is defined as an appraisal or investigation of a business, product or person.
As a rule of thumb, the more money you intend to spend, and the more critical new software, or a new service will be to your business, the more due diligence you should do.

When reviewing your final shortlist, you may find it helpful to gather the answers to some important questions:

- How can we find out more about the software vendors, consultancies or suppliers that we will be doing business with?
- Are the contracts (such as terms and conditions and EULAs) we will be bound by acceptable to us as a company?

If you are a smaller SME without teams to carry out these tasks, try to delegate these activities, or alternatively hire in specialists to help you with this aspect of the selection process.

The questions asked in Chapter 8 covered a lot of ground in terms of product and supplier suitability. Now, let's consider some other aspects of due diligence. You might also wish to consider the following:

Compatibility. How easy will it be to work with the company? Now that you've asked questions, sent emails and had telephone conversations, you should have an idea of how responsive and helpful each company is, and whether you feel you can work well together.

This will be particularly important if you're going to have a lot of configuration or customisation work done, or the company is going to be building your product for you.

Longevity. How well established is the service you intend to use?

Financial audit. It is fairly straightforward to research the financial standing of limited companies and to access information including their business structure, accounts, registered office address, trading age / date of incorporation and directors' names using online checking services.

You can also request company credit checks; usually including reports showing a company's credit score, credit limit, adverse information listed against the company and bankruptcy searches to confirm that the company has been stable for the last few years.

- *Endole* provide a company overview, list of directors and company filing history, http://www.endole.co.uk/.
- *Experian*, offers a similar service, http://www.experian.co.uk/Business-Express (UK) and www.experian.com/small-business/business-credit-reports.jsp (US / Canada).
- *Creditsafe,* provide business credit information, http://www.creditsafe.com/products/business-credit-reports, http://static.creditsafe.com/USAWebsite-demo/Content/Company/Search/Pages/CompanySearch.aspx?_ga=1.208843730.1155743831.1486078232 (US).
- *Creditserve,* can be used to assess the stability of businesses based in the UK and Europe, www.creditserve.co.uk/Products-and-Services/Online-overseas-company-search.
- *Companies House Beta site*, provides free company information, https://beta.companieshouse.gov.uk/.

Bankruptcy

You can cross-check the names of businesses and individuals using a number of online services, including:

- The *bankruptcy and insolvency register*: https://www.gov.uk/search-bankruptcy-insolvency-register.
- *The Insolvency Service*; https://www.insolvencydirect.bis.gov.uk/eiir/.
- *The National Archives*; http://www.nationalarchives.gov.uk/help-with-your-research/o-guides/bankrupts-insolvent-debtors/
- *The Accountants in Bankruptcy (AiB) in Scotland;* https://www.aib.gov.uk/debt/register-insolvencies.

Taking references

It's advisable to take up references that cover the performance of both the software and supplier with at least two companies, especially if you're purchasing a permanent license, or paying a large upfront fee for software and services. (This is less likely with SaaS contracts, which usually don't have long tie-ins.)

Ask the software supplier to arrange reference telephone calls (or site visits) with two of their customers, ideally with similar requirements to yours, that have been using the product for at least 3 months.

If they can supply references from companies of a similar size, and in a similar, or complementary sector, that will give you an insight into the benefits and challenges that companies like yours have experienced. Matching you up with direct competitors may not work as well because referees may feel uncomfortable discussing how they *really* use the product with a rival company.

Ask a combination of my **21** recommended reference questions and you will be *very* well informed before making your final decision!

1. How long have you had the product?
2. How many other companies / products did you consider? Which companies were these?
3. Why did you choose *this* company and *this* product? What "swung" the decision?
4. How smoothly did the implementation process go? (Did it take the expected amount of time, or longer? Did they experience any issues? How did they get over them?)
5. Did you complete the project within budget? (Ask how this was achieved, or what caused the project to run over budget.)
6. What's working well with the product and the supplier?
7. What hasn't gone so well?
8. How has the new software affected office life?
9. What are the biggest benefits you have experienced since getting the software?
10. Did you get all the benefits you had hoped to get from the product? (If yes, why do they think this is the case? How did they achieve this? If no, why not?)
11. What are the biggest challenges, or disadvantages that you have experienced with the software, or the vendor? (What's the history behind these issues and how / why did they arise?)
12. Have you achieved a return on your investment so far? (If so, how has this been achieved? If not, why do they think that is?

Will they be making any adjustments to help them achieve a ROI and what steps will they be taking?)

13. Do you think the product is good value for money?
14. How long did it take for your company to get used to using the product?
15. What training (if any) did you receive? (How would you rate the quality of the training? Why?)
16. Did you have to do much customisation to get the product to do what you wanted it to do? (How much time and money was required to achieve this? Was this more, or less than expected?)
17. How helpful has the supplier been in resolving your issues?
18. Do you pay for the technical support you receive? Would you consider it good value for money?
19. Have you had to involve any other parties in order to get the software up-and-running, or to enhance the product? Was this expected? (Find out who the parties were, what work was done, and why.)
20. What tips, or advice would you offer us as a company that is considering investing in software X and working with company Y?
21. If you had to start again from scratch, would you still select the same company and product? (What, if anything, would they do differently?)

Site visits

You may also wish to request a site visit to a data centre before deciding about a managed cloud service, or colocation service. Whether you visit or not, you may decide to check the security measures that exist for physical entry to the data centre.

These should include controlled entry to the site, multi-factor authentication (multiple checks of different types to confirm the identities of visitors), plus other security protocol including alarms, CCTV, motion sensors, restricted access areas and restrictions on items that can be brought into the data centre, in addition to security procedures for the prevention of cyber threats.

Contracts and agreements

As well as having strategic, functional, compliance and cost based deal-breakers, there may also be contractual deal-breakers.

Therefore, it's a good idea to contact a lawyer and to send them any EULAs (end-user license agreements), terms and conditions, statements of work (SOWs) or other contracts to review as quickly as possible once you know you are seriously considering a supplier or vendor, so they can identify unfavourable, or overly restrictive contract clauses, or even suggest new ones! Be prepared for some back and forth as you raise queries and negotiate.

ESCROW

What is ESCROW and when should you use it?

ESCROW offers several options for protecting your business.

Money or assets can be held in ESCROW by a neutral third-party (such as a bank, or specialist ESCROW agent) on your behalf during a business transaction, with the items held to be transferred (completing the transaction between buyer and seller) only once a set of agreed criteria have been fulfilled.

Source code ESCROW requires the *source code* for your software to be deposited with a third-party ESCROW agent. This action may protect you if there is long-term, or permanent disruption to your service because your software provider:

- Fails to update, or maintain their software
- Fails to deliver as per the terms of your agreement
- Goes bankrupt

If the terms of the ESCROW contract are breached, your company may be granted access to the source code and be free to host, develop and to continue to use the software.

It is also important to be aware of the downsides to this form of arrangement.

- ESCROW becomes more complex in the case of SaaS contracts, as the software is rented by you and owned by the vendor.
- Unless the version of the software held in ESCROW is up-to-date and comes with current, detailed documentation, *and* you enlist the skills of a developer, or team able to understand, maintain and develop the code, you may still experience issues with the software.

If the software is mission critical, this may still be a worthwhile measure. Seek legal advice if you are interested in establishing an ESCROW arrangement, and be sure to clarify how your data (and interests) will be protected if your software supplier suspends, or withdraws their service for any reason(s).

These points should be included in the terms of your ESCROW agreement.

Bespoke software, non-disclosure and intellectual property rights

If you intend to have software built to meet your needs, whether this is developed internally, or by consultants, you may wish to protect your business using an *NDA*, and to safeguard your *intellectual property rights, (IPR)*.

Intellectual property and confidentiality go hand-in-hand. Safeguard your right to any code developed and ensure that any persons called upon to advise you in matters related to your project, or involved in creating the software are not at liberty to discuss your plans.

Non-disclosure agreements (NDA's)

NDA's, (also described as secrecy or confidentiality agreements) require individuals or businesses to keep any ideas, material, knowledge, processes, or trade secrets (methods by which your business maintains its competitive advantage) they are party to confidential, giving you grounds to take action in court against those who break their terms. NDAs are either one way or two-way agreements:

- **One-way NDAs (also known as unilateral NDAs)** should be used when your business is the only party disclosing sensitive information.

- **Two-way NDAs (also known as a mutual or reciprocal NDAs)** should be used if both parties involved will be sharing information that they wish to remain confidential.

Pro Tip!

Take care to mark communications as confidential.

Businesses you may deal with, including professional services firms, financial advisers, insurance brokers, accountants, consultancies, business coaches, advisers, banks or 3rd party companies that are privy to information about your business are *not* automatically bound to keep your affairs private.

NDAs should only be signed by a person that has been authorised to sign contracts on behalf of your business and returned *before* information about your business or requirements are disclosed.

They may last for several years, but *can't* be enforced if the information becomes publicly available.

Ask the Expert – a legal perspective.

Non-disclosure Agreements (NDAs)

The NDA should broadly identify the reason why the information is being shared - for example, the parties will be exchanging confidential information for the purpose of evaluating the delivery of a software solution, or service.

Key points to look out for in NDAs include:

1. The duration of the contract (the contract term.)
2. The period for which the information should be kept confidential.
3. A requirement for the confidential information to be returned or destroyed; and
4. Ensuring that you do not warrant that the information you provide is accurate and complete in order to prevent claims being made against you.

The other party, or *counterparty,* may wish to share the confidential information with their professional advisors, but the NDA should state that the advisors should be subject to restrictions which are in line with those that you expect from the counterparty.

The UK government's gov.uk website has several versions of NDA available to view and download, along with tips and advice at: https://www.gov.uk/government/publications/non-disclosure-agreements.

SEQ Legal offer a selection of free and pay-as-you-go legal documents for IT, Internet and Business Law; http://www.seqlegal.com/.

If you're UK based, *Lawbite* offers access to an assortment of legal documents on a pay-as-you-go basis for a one off cost of £99 + VAT including e-signing facilities and two free fifteen minute legal advice sessions: https://www.lawbite.co.uk and *Rocket Lawyer* charges £25 a month for access to legal documents and the ability to ask questions; https://www.rocketlawyer.co.uk/.

It is still recommended that you seek legal advice to ensure that your contracts contain all the clauses and caveats relevant to your specific situation.

Intellectual Property (IP) and Intellectual Property Rights (IPR)

The transfer of IP is critical in order to protect your intellectual property rights.

IP is an umbrella term which covers copyrights, patents, designs and trademarks and the laws and codes of practice related to them.

Software is usually protected under **copyright law.**

The Intellectual Property Office (IPO), the government body responsible for intellectual property rights in the UK, provide information about patents and computer programs here:

http://www.ipo.gov.uk/blogs/iptutor/stem-patents-and-trade-secrets-part-1/.

This page from the IPO contains an IP overview, as well as links to other IP topics:
https://www.gov.uk/government/organisations/intellectual-property-office.

If you have paid for bespoke software to gain a competitive advantage, but do not own the source code, then ownership will remain with the company that built the software.

Under these circumstances, there will be nothing to legally prevent them from repackaging your ideas and selling these on to other companies in your industry, wiping out any advantage that you may have gained.

You will also be bound to them in terms of doing any further development or maintenance work, at whatever price they wish to charge for their services.

If the source code is yours, however, then any persons or organisations of your choosing may modify the code on your behalf.

Therefore, the agreement to transfer IP should be captured in writing in the form of a deed, or contract.

If a 3rd party is building the software for you, your contract should confirm *when* the source code will be transferred into your care and *how* it will be transferred.

Ask the Expert – a legal perspective

The transfer of intellectual property rights, IPR

It is important to distinguish between situations where:

1. The customer will <u>purchase and own </u>the software that has been developed for them, in which case the contract should require the vendor to provide the source code; and
2. The customer will <u>purchase a licence to use</u> the software that has been developed for them, where it follows that they may not receive the source code, and this may be a point of negotiation, depending on how the cost of the software development has been apportioned by the parties. (Please also refer to the ESCROW section in this chapter.)

In the case of point 1, the software vendor will normally request transfer of the IPR on receipt of payment. The customer should be aware that where there are staggered payment terms, they may not take ownership of the IPR until payment has been made in full.

The contract will typically contain a number of warranties that are given by the software developer, including that the software does not infringe a third party's IPR.

The customer may wish to seek specific indemnification from the vendor (or software developer) on this point, as an infringing product could prevent the customer from using the software, have significant cost implications and expose the customer to legal claims.

Given that financial liability under the contract is often capped at a maximum amount, the customer would therefore seek to:

- Exclude this indemnification from any financial cap on the vendor's liability that is set out in the *limitation of liability* clause in the vendor's contract, or
- Negotiate a higher financial limit that will apply to claims under the indemnity.

The software developer is unlikely to provide any warranties in relation to third party IPR for other software or services provided to the customer under a separate licence between the customer and any third-party licensor, for instance where one service enables or supports another, but where the two services are supplied by different software vendors.

Consequently, any claims the customer may have in relation to the third party IPR will need to be brought against the licensor of that third party IPR, and not the vendor.

Employment contracts and IPR

Who owns the intellectual property generated by an employee working for your business?

Most businesses will be keen to protect their ideas and assert ownership of the source code for any software that is developed, along with any other IP linked with a project of this type.

Under the *UK Patents Act 1977*, the default ownership of an invention lies with the *employer*, rather than the employee, even if this is not explicitly included in an employment contract. This is also the case in Australia, however ownership rights are less clear-cut in the US. However, the inclusion of clauses related to new inventions, processes and discoveries in employment contracts is a wise precaution which will help you to guard against future misunderstandings!

Ask the Expert – a legal perspective.

Intellectual property rights in the workplace

Under English law, the general rule is that the <u>employer</u> will own all IPR that is produced by its <u>employees</u> in the course of their employment. As a starting point, the employer of a developer will own all the IPR in the code they write.

The grey area here is "in the course of their employment" and employers should be aware of developers who work on their own ad hoc projects during their period of employment.
Most employers will want to avoid the developer making use of their confidential and proprietary information for their own use, or potentially creating a competing product.

If the employee is employed outside of the UK, then local laws will apply: the employment contract should clearly set out the position on IPR ownership to the extent that the local laws allow.
The employment contract is also the right place to set out:

- Restrictions on the use of confidential information and trade secrets.
- Details of IPR ownership
- The extent to which the developer can work on their own projects, and
- Any restrictive covenants which will prevent them from competing with the employer for a specified period.

The opposite is true of <u>contractors or consultants</u> who will own the IPR in the work created by them, even if it is carried out under a contract for services for a third party, unless the contract states otherwise.
A well drafted consultancy agreement will deal with IPR ownership and provide for the contractor to transfer all of the IPR in the work to the company that has engaged them to provide the services.

Service Level Agreements

A *Service Level Agreement (SLA),* is a contract between
a service provider and the recipient of the services.
It defines the level of service that a customer will receive, including:

- Service targets and response times
- Service uptime / availability
- Hours of operation
- Duties and responsibilities
- Inclusions and exclusions
- Escalation procedures
- Notice periods (on both sides)
- Conditions under which the contract can be terminated
- Limits and restrictions
- Penalties if the terms of the SLA are not met

Ask to see a copy of the SLA and Terms of Business for each company on your
final shortlist and read ALL the small print!

Don't be shy about asking for the agreement to be modified if you don't like
what you see. If the supplier refuses, you must decide how comfortable you
feel about having a business relationship with them.

Pro tip

SLAs and breaches of contract.

Keep track of dates and times of outages and their duration.
You may have grounds to break your contract if the terms of your SLA ar
being breached –
or you may be due a rebate, or compensation.
Before making any commitments, confirm that there are penalty clauses
SLA. I have seen
businesses in completely powerless positions with SLAs that do not cont
penalty clauses.
There was no incentive for the supplier to improve their service and no
recourse for the company,
who were tied into a contract without any bargaining chips.

> Be prepared to request penalty clauses to cover poor service, including f
> to meet adequate standards of service or quality.
> If necessary, engage the services of a lawyer to negotiate on your
> behalf.

Before signing a contract for managed or colocation services, check on the *service uptime* commitments (please refer to Chapter 8 for information about uptime) made by Cloud Service providers in their Service Level Agreements (SLAs), and confirm the availability of their support teams.
Are they available 24 hours a day, 7 days a week, 365 days a year?

Other documents and contractual agreements

We discussed the Statement of Work, or SOW back in Chapter 7. Review this, and any other documents such as project, implementation, or rollout plans, and query any points that still require clarification, or amendment before moving forward.
If certain items are particularly important to you as a business, consider asking for these to be made part of a formal contract.

Proof of concept (POC) / creating a prototype

A *proof of concept,* or *prototype* requires a greater commitment than just making the time to test out potential products. A "POC" generally has a cost attached to it because it involves a supplier customising and / or configuring their product for you, typically with a subset of your business data migrated into it, so you can test the product in a life-like environment.

A POC can be a very sensible investment, especially if a product is costly. It is far better to pay for a POC, or prototype to help you to decide whether an option is worth pursuing, than to pay for a full-scale version of the software, only to find that it does not live up to expectations.

Running a POC will allow you to road-test a potential supplier, *and* their product.
You will be testing the feasibility and practicality of your proposed plans, and the process of copying a subset of your data into the new system - a

useful preview of the work to come in migrating *all* your business data across to the new software.

Having worked with the supplier, you will be able to see how they operate (and communicate) with you as a customer and you can decide whether you wish to develop a longer-term relationship with them based on your experiences.

The key objectives, scope and duration of this mini-project will need to be agreed, and some staff will need to be assigned to work on testing the product and providing feedback during the POC.

Once concluded, a meeting to review the success of the POC and to discuss feedback, next steps, and lessons learned usually takes place. These lessons are then considered when configuring / customising the full product.

Now you've completed your *verbal, visual, manual, written,* and *due-diligence* checks, you may be ready to choose your new product!

In the next chapter, we'll review ways to improve your chances of achieving a rapid ROI, as you transition from the selection process to preparing to embed new software into your business.

References

The UK Government. *What IP is.* https://www.gov.uk/intellectual-property-an-overview/what-ip-is.

The IPO: http://www.ipo.gov.uk.

Legislation.gov.uk, *The UK Patents Act 1977.* http://www.legislation.gov.uk/ukpga/1977/37

Queensland Government. *Do I own intellectual property that my employees create?* https://www.business.qld.gov.au/running-business/protecting-business/ip-kit/browse-ip-topics/ownership-of-intellectual-property-created-by-your-employees-and-contractors-or-consultants/ownership

CHAPTER 10

Minimising risk, maximising ROI: how to successfully implement your new software

"Perhaps the complaint we hear most frequently from executives…is that they haven't realized much business value from the high-priced technology they have installed. Meanwhile, the list of seemingly necessary IT capabilities continues to grow, and IT spending continues to consume an increasing percentage of their budgets. Where's the payback?"

- Harvard Business Review

This comment was made in **2002** and these challenges are *still* as relevant to businesses today as they were back then!

Throughout this book, I have been referring to ways to ensure that you achieve a good return on your investment.

You know that every decision that you make will play a role in establishing how much of a return on investment you achieve and how rapidly this happens.

However, it's important not only to make good decisions, but also to take preventative action and manage risks. Problems with your software may drain time, create disruption, possibly lead to more expense, and make it harder to achieve a good ROI.

In this chapter, we'll talk about ways to reduce the chances of problems occurring with your new software and we'll review all the measures you can take to make sure your investment pays dividends.

Are you ready to "go live" with your new software?

Let's begin with a word of warning. If your software is rolled-out prematurely, you are more likely to experience issues with your product.

Consider the following questions before going ahead with a software implementation:

- **Are all the technical, functional and non-functional items on your "must" list in place?** If there is any functionality that is not yet configured or customised are you happy to go ahead and switch over to the new software, or would it be better to wait? If so, what workarounds or temporary measures will you put in place until all your functionality is ready?
  If you need more bandwidth, a more advanced database, or specific hardware or software to optimise the performance of the new system and these technical specifications are not in place before go-live, you may experience problems.
- **Has the product been tested as an entire system?** Does the whole product operate as expected? Is it stable and free of bugs and significant issues? Is the product successfully integrated with any other tools, or software as agreed? Have all integrations, or connections between products been tested?
- **Has the feedback from your user acceptance testing, (UAT) been positive?**
  UAT confirms that a product is acceptable to the group who are going to be using it.
  It is a chance for the future recipients of the software to attempt to use it as they would in the real-world, and to report on its performance.
  If you've received feedback which suggests that more work needs to be done, there is no point going ahead without considering what this feedback is telling you, and what action(s) should be taken before the product can be used. The more rounds of UAT you complete, the more issues you will be able to identify and resolve and the less problems you are likely to face once the new software is "rolled out."
- **Do you have a plan for training - and for minimising disruption in the office?** Put a schedule in place, taking into account the number of people to be trained, the duration of the training and how many people can be trained per session. Does a rota need to be set up

with some staff assigned to maintain essential business activities, whilst others receive training?

- **Have you set a date, or check-point to assess your readiness?** The decision to go ahead with a software roll-out is often determined by choosing a realistic date and holding a Go / No-go meeting where the aspects of readiness, both in terms of systems, people and processes will be discussed. A decision will be made to go ahead, or not. If it is not deemed safe to go ahead, then a date should be set for another meeting with objectives set to rectify the issues identified at the initial meeting.

Transitioning to a new system (the implementation process)

There are 4 main ways to introduce new software into your business. You may choose:

A parallel rollout. This is a much lower risk approach than killing off your old system and switching straight over to a new one!

In this scenario, you maintain your old systems and keep them running for a period of time (a few weeks, to a few months or more) after the new software is in place. This is a prudent way to safeguard your business operations because your old system still exists as a backup. You can also validate the accuracy of the *new* software by checking that calculations or data outputs are the same across both systems.

On the downside, this means supporting two systems from a financial perspective, plus extra effort from staff, who may need to input the same data into both systems (called *double-keying*) to keep them both up-to-date.

Usually all the data up to a specified date will be loaded into the new system and then from there, both systems will need to be updated manually, or via a feed between them to keep them both synchronised. (Convenient, but probably a chargeable extra.)

Once you feel confident that the new software can run your operations, you can retire the old system. Alternatively, if there are issues, you might choose to leave the *old system* in place for a longer period.

A phased rollout. You may also wish to phase in the new software and phase out the old in stages. This can be done in different ways - team by team, or office by office for instance, with a schedule in place, clear instructions for staff, and a plan for minimising confusion whilst some groups are using the old software and others have switched over to the new.

A pilot rollout. A pilot rollout involves trialling the product in isolation for a period of time, for instance with one team. If the pilot proves to be successful, the software is rolled out to all users.

With the *pilot, phased* and *parallel rollout strategies*, there is an opportunity to observe the new system "in action," to note any issues that occur and to adjust it whilst the old system is still running.

A direct cutover, or immediate rollout, which involves "pulling the plug" on your old system and having a "hard" switch-over between one system and the other without any transition period.

This approach carries the highest risk. There may be no way back in terms of restoring the old system and although the new one should have been tested prior to the rollout, there will be no fallback position to shield your business from any unforeseen issues that arise.

If you are replacing business-critical software, don't expose yourself to unnecessary risk.

Speak to your software vendor and explore the options available. My professional preference is to have a plan A, B and even C in place in case issues arise!

Training
You will struggle to get *any* ROI if training is inadequate - the potential

of your software can't be fully realised without it!

Do everything you can to make sure staff *understand* how to use it and *like* using it. (This is one of the points where selection of a product without involving stakeholders may come back to bite you.)

Quality training will also minimise disruption within your business.

If staff have been well trained and know what they are doing, you will have a much smoother time transitioning to the new system.

Here are **10** ways to get the maximum benefits from staff training:

1. Allow adequate time for training. You will *not* get the best from staff who are using a system that they don't understand.

Don't rush, or cut corners when it comes to training - this sends out the message that learning is not a priority.

2. Have a set of training resources available in different formats to support different learning styles. There is a large body of research that confirms that we all have preferred learning styles. These can vary considerably between people, so it is a good idea to have training materials that allow staff to learn through observation and hands-on practical training, as well as via other methods.

Regardless of who does the training, make sure there will be sufficient opportunities for staff to ask questions and ensure that a range of materials will be made available for staff to use.

In Chapter 8 we grilled service providers about the quality and variety of training materials available for this precise reason. More formats increase the chances that people will find a mode of learning that suits them, which makes for a deeper understanding of the tool.

3. Make sure training is contextual and relevant. Examples and scenarios provided during training should relate to the specifics of employees' daily tasks and activities. Pointing out in abstract terms that "this button here does this", or "that option there will do that", without any reference to practical, real-world scenarios is not necessarily good enough.

4. Reinforce best-practice as part of the training, including expected behaviours and ways of working. New systems represent a new phase in the life of a company and this is a great time to:

- Engage staff and make sure that everyone understands your vision and how they fit into it.
- Revisit compliance procedures, regulations and company policies; linking them back to processes and activities in the new system.
- Reinforce the importance of policies and processes. Explain why they are so important, and communicate the consequences of non-compliance for your staff and your business.

5. Be prepared to offer refresher and mop-up training sessions to staff. Do not attach any stigma to requesting refresher training. It is far better to allow staff to repeat training so they can be productive, than to have people unable to perform at their best because they did not grasp everything the first time. Repetition is an important part of learning, so allow scope for refreshing staff's knowledge to help them to reinforce what they have learned. *Repeating sessions will also be useful to train new recruits who had not joined when the initial training took place, or staff who were absent when others received their training.*

6. Select staff to act as super users or power users. Most businesses, or teams have at least one person who knows how to fix the printer, resolve technical issues and is the go-to person when these sorts of problems arise. Who is yours?
Consider asking them to become an advanced user of the system, able to help and support other staff.
Having internal super users reduces your reliance on external help. Multiple in-house experts can share super user responsibilities more easily, reducing the risk of you losing skills and knowledge if your sole super user were to leave your company. Allow additional time for super users to be trained and give them a head-start in learning how to use the product.
Super users may also be trained to manage configuration tasks, further reducing your reliance on your software provider. You may save money on fees and have changes made more quickly, but you will also need to consider the impact on super users' normal duties.

7. Make sure staff know exactly where to access training resources. If there are self-service resources available, make them as easy to access as possible. The harder it is to access learning aides, the less motivated staff will be to hunt for the information, even if they need it. This may lead to people taking shortcuts, or falling into bad habits.

8. Consider creating your own knowledge base. This will help you retain knowledge within your business as existing staff leave and new employees join.

If all questions raised (and the answers to them) are captured, you will be able to build a very useful internal resource. Categorise the information by topic to make it more accessible. This resource will also reduce the impact on your business when any of your super users leave your company. One page "cheat sheets" with reminders and tips and other easy-access training materials will also be incredibly helpful for your staff. Depending on your policy about paper in the office and assuming there is no sensitive information on the cheat sheet, allow people to pin these up or put them in prominent places to help them as they work.

9. Set up a communications channel that makes it easy for staff to raise issues with a line manager, team leader or super user.

Encourage staff to make suggestions and continue to fine-tune processes until they are optimal. This will have a positive effect on your ROI, will speed up your time to value (TTV), and increase staff's morale and enthusiasm. Make sure staff know who they should contact if they have a question, or issue. Set up an email mailbox for feedback and comments, or organise them in an electronic file, or desktop folder and regularly transfer questions raised, and answers provided across to your knowledge base.

10. Be prepared to troubleshoot. Be ready to chase the software vendor or service provider if necessary. For best results, you'll need them to provide answers quickly, so that staff aren't inconvenienced and do not develop a negative impression of the product. It's best to manage expectations, so explain that a few teething troubles might arise early on, but this is no cause for alarm.

Support your super users in the event of any issues arising, and check that they are freed up and ready to help people, especially in the first few weeks after the new software has been rolled out.

Project management

The Project Plan

If you are having software built by a 3rd party, or are buying software that needs to be customised or configured by a supplier, then the vendors' personnel will usually draw up a project plan.

This should include; the objectives of the project, inclusions and exclusions, a schedule of activities, named owners of tasks, and due dates. Depending on the work that is to be done, the plan may include the following tasks and activities:

- **Set-up, or initiation tasks** to get the project started.
- **Build, or customisation** work – this will cover any development work and code-based adjustments to be made to the product.
- **Configuration** - any manual adjustments to menus, settings, options, or other elements of the software that are required.
- **Data migration and testing** - the work to be done to transfer your data into the new system and to confirm that the transfer was successful.
- **System testing** - testing of the whole system, including all its functionality and processes.
- **Integration testing** - to test how different software products operate together as a coordinated whole, and to check for any issues with stability, reliability or "weak links" between 3rd party software, systems or services working alongside each other to deliver or receive information.
- **UAT -** User Acceptance Testing allows the intended users of the system to evaluate the work that external consultants have done and to check that all the required processes are present and correct. UAT can also help staff get familiar with new systems, as well as providing valuable feedback on what is, and isn't working as expected.
- **Installation / implementation** - this will confirm the "roll-out" plan for moving from the old system to the new one, as discussed earlier in this chapter.

- **Training** - confirming when, where and how staff will be trained, and the topics to be covered.
- **Significant dates** - including key milestones or check-points.

Tracking progress

If you wish to keep track of progress and delivery milestones, a simple Excel project plan can be set up. You may wish to:

- List tasks or *deliverables* in the first column.
- List the *people* who need to action the tasks in the second column.
- Put the *status* of each task in the 3rd column (pending, in progress, complete, overdue, etc.)
- Map the task's *duration* over the correct number of days, weeks or months, by highlighting the relevant fields in Excel.

Fig 13 - Microsoft Project could be used, but may require training, making Excel an easier solution. Work plan template, Tools4dev.org.

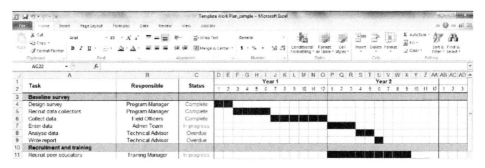

Project management skills

Do you have a project management function within your business?

Ideally, there should be at least one nominated person who can coordinate activities internally and act as a point of contact between your business and any 3rd parties that you are dealing with.

This nominated person may also check that things are progressing according to the plans and agreements in place (and chase people if this is not the case!), keep track of deadlines, identify risks to the project and report on progress to the relevant people within your business. (You might consider assigning key responsibilities to different staff members as an alternative plan.)

Let's review some simple tips and tools to aid with project and risk management.

Shielding your project from risks

The person wearing the project management (PM) "hat" should think like a pessimist. When operating in project manager mode, they will regularly need to consider worst-case scenarios.

This is not overly negative, or cautious - resolving (and being prepared) for problems is a key part of the PM role.

Risks have the potential to turn into issues that can harm projects, so it is important to consider them. To avoid becoming overwhelmed by a large number of project risks, PMs usually categorise risks and deal with them according to priority.

Managing and mitigating risks

To assess project risks, you'll need to consider the following:

- What might go wrong? List all the issues you can think of.
- What is the *probability* or *likelihood* that each item on your list might happen? Low, medium or high? Put a likelihood rating against each risk.
- How badly might your project be affected if the worst were to happen? Would the *impact* on your project be low, medium or high? Put a likelihood rating against each risk.

Review your list and prioritise the risks based on likelihood and impact, assigning them to one of the 4 quadrants shown in the diagram in fig 13.

Next, do a quick brainstorming exercise and note down some solutions or alternative courses of action to help you deal with the risks. Start with the risks that are the most likely to occur, with the highest impact. Begin with the orange quadrant (top left), followed by the blue quadrant (bottom left) and then the green quadrant (top right). The purple quadrant (bottom right) should be the very lowest priority.

Fig 14 - Risk and impact assessment quadrant.
https://opentextbc.ca/projectmanagement/wp-content/uploads/sites/3/2014/06/risk-and-impact.jpg

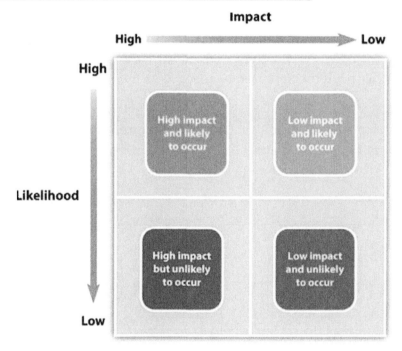

What solutions did you come up with?

The options for managing your risks will typically fall into one of 4 categories:

Avoid. Risks can be avoided, or prevented, by pursuing safer alternatives. For example, adjusting, or simplifying your approach in places where your plan looks like it may be more challenging than first expected. Another example of risk avoidance would be to rule out working with a 3rd party that has a bad reputation or slow response times.

Mitigate. Lessen the impact of a risk by taking action. Taking out business insurance is a form of risk mitigation, as is running due diligence checks on a vendor, or service provider.

Transfer. You might choose to transfer risk by outsourcing it. You'll still need to be confident that the 3rd party that you're transferring the risk to can do a respectable job on your behalf. Otherwise, choosing to work with them will just add *another* risk to your list!

Accept. You may choose to proceed knowing that certain risks exist that you cannot avoid, mitigate or transfer. Despite this you can still make sure you fully understand the possible negative outcomes associated with the risk. Monitor the risk and take any actions that might neutralise it if the opportunity arises.

Fig 15. Risk management options. By Barron & Barron Project Management for Scientists and Engineers, http://cnx.org/content/col11120/1.4/.

| Avoid | Mitigate | Transfer | Accept |

Now follow through, and take actions to mitigate your highest priority risks based on the ideas you came up with.

Because situations and circumstances change during projects, it's worth repeating the risk assessment process. The more rapidly things are changing, the more frequently you should review your risks.

This marks the end of the book!

For best results, ask questions and probe beneath the surface when assessing software, vendors and services, consider people, as well as processes, and ensure that your requirements are clear and well prioritised, so that you can make the right decisions for your business.

The next chapter contains a number of SME-friendly software products, many of which are free, or low cost. A few pages beyond that, there is a list of all the templates and documents provided free with this book.

Thank you for reading. I hope you have found this software survival guide both helpful, and informative!

If you have any queries, I offer several free telephone and Skype sessions to readers of my books each month. You can contact me at: hello@purposefulgroup.com, or http://www.purposefulgroup.com/contact-us.html

---

References

Harvard Business Review (HBR). *Six IT Decisions Your IT People Shouldn't Make.* https://hbr.org/2002/11/six-it-decisions-your-it-people-shouldnt-make.

Decision Sciences Journal of Innovative Education; *Using Learning Style Instruments to Enhance Student Learning.* Thomas F. Hawk, Amit J. Shah. http://onlinelibrary.wiley.com/doi/10.1111/j.1540-4609.2007.00125.x/full.

Psychological Science in the Public Interest. An official journal of the Association for Psychological Science. *Learning Styles; Concepts and*

Evidence. Harold Pashler, Mark McDaniel, Doug Rohrer, Robert Bjork. http://journals.sagepub.com/doi/abs/10.1111/j.1539-6053.2009.01038.x.

CHAPTER 11

Free and low-cost small business tools

There are many useful, free or low-cost, cloud-based software applications targeted at the SME market. I have used, or trialled some of the products listed here myself.

As always, do your checks, make enquiries and take advantage of any free trials available to help you assess product suitability. Please note that prices, websites and the products themselves are subject to change.

Accountancy software
Xero; https://www.xero.com/uk/, or https://www.xero.com.

Sage accounting software; http://uk.sageone.com/.

Freshbooks; https://www.freshbooks.com/uk (UK), https://www.freshbooks.com/ (US).

Business intelligence / Analytics

Kissmetrics, describe their service as one that allows businesses to "track and understand what people are doing and take action to accelerate your growth." https://www.kissmetrics.com/products/.

Mixpanel offers "instant insights for everyone on mobile and web." https://mixpanel.com.

Coordination and communication
Whether your team is based in the same office, or in different locations, these tools will help them stay in sync and increase visibility of the tasks being performed. Slack is a popular instant messaging tool for teams which includes document sharing. Slack offers a free version of their tool that comes with 5 GB of document storage, a 10k data allowance of searchable messages and call functionality for up to 2 people: https://slack.com.

Trello, is an excellent tool, it is flexible and can be used for many business activities including project management, team organisation, task, and issue tracking: https://trello.com/.

I've prepared some Trello boards that you can copy and adapt for your own use. You will find links to them on the *Resources* page.

Basecamp provides online project management capabilities: https://basecamp.com/.

Bitrix24 includes a social network, video and chat, task and calendar management and a CRM (Customer Relationship Management system): https://www.bitrix24.com/.

Customer services & support
Fresh desk: https://freshdesk.com.

Trello is also flexible enough to manage customer service queries. (See the links above.)

Zendesk provides helpdesk management software. There's a free trial available for each price package: https://www.zendesk.com/product/pricing/#faqs.

Document creation and management
Google's *G Suite* for business, covers emails that can be sent from your own domain (and not @gmail.com), calendar management, spread sheets, document processing, and presentations: https://gsuite.google.com/.

Zoho also offers a range of document creation tools, including word processing, spread sheets and presentations: https://www.zoho.com/docs/#.

Issue tracking and task management software for development teams
Mingle: https://www.thoughtworks.com/mingle/ and

JIRA; https://jira.atlassian.com/secure/Dashboard.jspa are specialist task management and tracking systems used to store project requirements.

Trello: https://trello.com/.

These tools allow work to be assigned to team members and can also be used as issue tracking tools. Trello and Mingle are both freemium products - both have a free basic version.

Meetings, video and chat
Skype: https://web.skype.com/en/.

GoToMeeting; online meeting software and screen sharing www.gotomeeting.com

Cisco WebEx: http://www.webex.co.uk, both allow one-to-one (and three-way) video conferences on their free plans.

HipChat. Group chat and instant messaging: https://www.hipchat.com.

Zoom. Video and web conferencing: https://zoom.us/.

Slack - see above.

Project management
Bitrix24, Trello, BaseCamp, or Excel can be used to store project plans.

Social media management
If you're seeking centralised control for social media posts, then *Hootsuite* will allow you to connect and post to up to 3 social media sites from a choice of Instagram, Facebook, Twitter, LinkedIn, Google+ and YouTube. There's a dashboard available to monitor your activity. Here's a link to their free service: https://hootsuite.com/create-free-account.

Buffer app covers all the social media sites serviced by Hootsuite, except for YouTube, https://buffer.com/pricing.

Pair this up with another social media tool like Likeable Hub (Facebook, Twitter and LinkedIn), https://likeablehub.com/ or Everypost, http://everypost.me/pricing/ to cover a large number of social media sites at once.

Edgar, described as "the social media queue that fills itself" is a more expensive tool, which will automatically recycle posts for you: https://meetedgar.com.

Suite applications
Zoho is mentioned under *Document Storage*, but this international company offers a wide range of SaaS applications for business; including a CRM product: https://www.zoho.com/crm/help/understanding-zohocrm.html, sales products, email services, website builder tools, presentation software, reporting, finance, helpdesk and HR software. You can find details about the whole product-suite here: https://www.zoho.com/.

Organisation and management of business processes
Wunderlist: https://www.wunderlist.com/.

Process Street. Checklist and workflow management software: http://www.process.st/v2/

Please see the *Next Steps* on the following page.

NEXT STEPS

What comes next?

1. Use the free resources that come with this book. The download links are on the next page.

2. Kindly leave me a review on Amazon, or Goodreads. *I would appreciate it greatly!*
You can do this by clicking the *Write a customer review* button on your local Amazon sales page for the book:
https://www.amazon.com/dp/B06XG1XFL7 (US), or
https://www.amazon.co.uk/dp/B06XG1XFL7 (UK).
myBook.to/small-business-software-buyers-guide (Universal link for all countries.)
https://www.goodreads.com/book/show/34501211-don-t-buy-software-for-your-small-business-until-you-read-this-book

Reviews help new readers to discover this book and decide whether they should read it. They will also help me to improve future editions of this book. Thanks in advance!

3. Spread the word. If you have friends, family or co-workers who would find this book helpful, please share the links below, or Tweet or post to social media:
https://www.amazon.com/dp/B06XG1XFL7, or myBook.to/small-business-software-buyers-guide (for all countries.)

4. Continue reading! If you enjoyed this book, my books about entrepreneurship and product development, and building software from scratch may be of interest to you. You can find out more about them in the pages at the front of the book.

ABOUT THE AUTHOR

K.N. Kukoyi is a Software Delivery Specialist and consultant who has spent more than a decade helping small businesses, multinationals and publicly listed companies to buy, build and launch their web and mobile apps from scratch as an Agile project manager, business analyst and software tester. The author became a Certified Scrum Master in 2008 and has Diplomas in Internet marketing and performance coaching.

She is the founder of Purposeful Products, a consultancy that solves software and business process related challenges, and helps clients to transform their ideas into software products.

hello@purposefulgroup.com
www.purposefulgroup.com

CREDITS

	Chapter 2
1	Fig 1 - Efficiency vs effectiveness grid. Author's own.
2	Fig 2 - A more complex chart by, from supplier to customer and the movement Of data, created using LucidChart. https://www.lucidchart.com.
	Chapter 3
3	Fig 3 - Public and private cloud hosting options. Author's own.
4	Fig 4 - inside a data centre. Credit. Global Access Point.
	Chapter 4
5	Fig 5 - Sequential and parallel tasks. Author's own.
	Chapter 5
6	Fig 6 - TCO calculator. http://www.softwareadvice.com/tco/#top.
7	Fig 7 - SharePoint CRM (On-premises) vs. Salesforce.com CRM (SaaS). http://www.sharepointcrmtemplate.com/blog/wp-content/uploads/2014/11/SPCRM-and-Salesforce-TCO-resized-600.png Source: SharePoint Flex: http://sharepointflex.com
8	Fig 8 - Very small business vs. Medium sized business. http://erpcloudnews.com/2011/03/erp-software-cost-comparison-on-premise-saas-and-hosted/.
9	Fig 9 - Very small business vs. Medium sized business. http://erpcloudnews.com/2011/03/erp-software-cost-comparison-on-premise-saas-and-hosted/.
10	Fig 10 - Auto enrolment staging dates. https://www.gov.uk/government/news/new-timetable-clarifies-automa enrolment-starting-dates.
11	Fig 11 - Sending personal data outside the European Economic Area (Principle 8): https://ico.org.uk/for-organisations/guide-to-data-protection/principle-8-international/.

Printed in Great Britain
by Amazon